T0078376

THE HEART OF OBEDIENCE

SHARON SPIKNER

authorHOUSE®

AuthorHouse™
1663 Liberty Drive
Bloomington, IN 47403
www.authorhouse.com
Phone: 833-262-8899

Published by AuthorHouse 05/25/2021

ISBN: 978-1-6655-1401-9 (sc)
ISBN: 978-1-6655-1408-8 (e)

Library of Congress Control Number: 2021900982

Print information available on the last page.

CONTENTS

DEDICATION

To Jesus Christ, my Lord and savior, who called me to ministry. To you be all the glory and honor forever and ever.

ACKNOWLEDGEMENT

I thank our Lord and savior Jesus Christ for giving me the strength and ability to write about obedience. Everything I am and I have is as a result of obeying God. I have been willing and obedient so I am eating the good of the land (Isaiah 1:19). Thank you Lord.

My grandmother, Cornie Armour and mother, Pastor Verlean McGhee, whose faith I inherited. Thank you for building a legacy of faith and obedience our generation. Without your nurturing, this book would not have been written.

I want to appreciate my daughter, Jasmine Spikner, son, Jeremy Spikner and grandchildren, Kinsley and Kimora, for allowing me to focus on writing this book.

Dimeji, thank you for believing and obeying God for joining me to do kingdom work. Your inspiration, insight and editing of this book are highly appreciated. God will yet do great work through you.

INTRODUCTION

This book is the story of my life. It's about the way I have walked with God since I accepted His call to ministry. I have seen my mother walked in obedience to the Lord.

When you pick this book to read, you will find something interesting. And that is obedience to the Lord Jesus Christ. Jesus was elevated to the highest position because of His obedience. Even though He was the Son of God yet He had to learn obedience by the things He suffered. God elevated Him and gave Him a name that is above every other name in heaven, on earth and in hell. Jesus became our Lord and Savior by obeying God and doing His will.

If we want to experience the life and blessings of God, then we need to follow the footsteps of Jesus and obey God. Obedience is the fruit of the spirit, while disobedience is the fruit of the flesh. We are commanded to walk in the spirit always.

We will only get the promise of God when we obey His instructions and commandments. They are meant to take us into His will and give us all that He has prepared for us in His kingdom.

We can only access the life of God when we walk in obedience. I believe this is the word that the Church needs to hear in this time. Many of us are walking in disobedience to the voice of God and as a result are outside His will. We need to get back into the will of God for our lives.

You may not know the will of God for your life right now. I believe this book will serve as a guide. If you will just decide to obey God even in small matters, He will lead you to His will for your life.

As you read this, I pray that the spirit of obedience and excellence will come upon you and God will rise upon you in power and the world will know He called and blessed you. The blessing is the fruit of obedience. To love the Lord with your heart is to obey Him. If you love God, obey His commandments and instruction. This is what living in the kingdom is.

I pray for grace upon your life to begin to walk in obedience and enter into the will of God for your life. There you will find blessing and rest for your soul.

Apostle Sharon Spikner

CHAPTER ONE

Imagination of the Heart

Noah had a difficult time. Everyone around him was against God. The imagination of men's heart was filled with wickedness. Yet God saw that the heart of Noah was different. His heart was filled with righteousness.

You will never understand what Noah went through until you find yourself among people who do not care about the things of God. The imaginations of their hearts are filled with wickedness not righteousness.

God saw the heart of Noah and called him to build the Art. He made a covenant with him. God called him out of the world to prepare him and send him back to the world as their deliverer. Noah accepted and obeyed God's call.

Genesis 7:1 (KJV) says, "And the Lord said unto Noah, come thou and all thy house into the ark; for thee have I seen righteous before me in this generation."

A generation means group of people born and living at about the same time. Which may mean 20 to 30 years during which children are born and grown up. It's a lifecycle of an organism from generation to generation.

Throughout the whole world God only found one man righteous and that was Noah.Its my prayer that God will find you righteous and faithful to call you into His assignment as He did Noah. What does God sees when He look down from heaven at man today? Will He see you as a righteous man?

You need to understand that God doesn't see as we men see. We focus on the outward appearance. That makes it really easy for us to be deceived. But no one can deceive God. He sees the heart. Whatever you are in your heart, that is who you really are. All your actions proceed from what is going on in your heart.

We are known by our fruits which is the product of what is happening in our heart. When God saw the heart of men, he knew that its just a matter of time before the whole earth gets covered in wickedness and people completely forget him.

We can only obey God, when we the imagination of our heart is filled with righteousness. However, when everyone imagines wickedness, the whole earth will be covered with wickedness and no one will want to obey God.

Obedience to God will become outdated and no one will want to do that. God doesn't want that to happen. Imagine a world where everyone imagines wickedness rather than righteousness.

Then the Lord saw that the wickedness of man was great in the earth, and that every intent of the thoughts of his heart was only evil continually. And the Lord was sorry that He had made man on the earth, and He was grieved in His heart. So the Lord said, "I will destroy man whom I have created from the face of the earth, both man and beast, creeping thing and birds of the air, for I am sorry that I have made them." But Noah found grace in the eyes of the Lord. Genesis 6:5-8 NKJV

There is a similarity between what God did with Noah and Jesus. At the time they both came, most people were not obeying God. The heart of men was filled with wickedness. Noah was chosen to preserve the righteousness of God. God knows that Noah will obey Him no matter what.

Jesus came when the earth was filled with corruption. Most people have lost connection and relationship with God. There was no one whose heart was right with God who walk in obedience to God. Jesus was sent to preserve humanity.

God chose Noah to build an Ark as He destroys sin and wickedness on God. He also sent Jesus to take away sin and destroy the works of the devil.

And you know that He was manifested to take away our sins, and in Him there is no sin. He who sins is of the devil, for the devil has sinned from the beginning. For this purpose the Son of God was manifested, that He might destroy the works of the devil. 1 John 3:5, 8NKJV

We as believers should be asking God to give us a new heart and put a new spirit within us.This is the word of the Lord: I will take the heart of stone out of your flesh and give you a heart of flesh. God is going to remove the rebellious, disobedience stubborn nature from our flesh and give us a new covenant heart to serve and obey and become His children.

The greatest thing that God requires from all of us is that we imagine His word and obey His voice. That way we get to produce heaven on earth (Read Ecclesiastes 12:13).

Because of Noah, his whole family was secured under grace that was given by God.What is grace? It is the love and mercy given to us by God because God desires us to have it, not necessarily because of anything we have done to earn it, it is not a created substance of any kind.

It is an attribute of God that is most manifest in the salvation of righteous man and sinner man. It's God unmerited mercy (favor) that God gave to humanity by sending His Son, Jesus Christ, to die on the cross which secure man's eternal salvation from sin.

Just imagine if the generation in Noah's days knew of the grace of God, will they have changed? God gave His grace to one family, a family saved by grace. Grace was looking for someone to comply; to obey. To comply means to yield, assent to, accord, agree or acquiesce, to adapt oneself;

to consent or conform, while obey is to do as an ordered by a person or institution, to act according to the bidding, to do as one is told to do in obedience.

This is to say that when God saw that the evil and the wickedness of man was great in the earth as it's in our generations today and that every imagination of our heartsare only evil continually, He decided to look for a man who can obey Him.Do we love the things of God? God was looking for a righteous man; a man after His heart. But Noah found grace in the eyes of the Lord.

The world today is more a replica of the times that Noah lived. The wickedness on earth today can only make Noah's time feel like child's play.

I think the plan is to get an idealism that stands against the knowledge of God such that obedience to God becomes something no one wants to do. One that will make everyone to obey the rules of government rather than obeying God.

It's contrary to the will of God. However, we all know that the counsel and will of God will always stand against any plan of humans. God is in the business of multiplying people on earth to do His will and bring His kingdom to the earth.

Show The Manifold Wisdom of God

God always sends us warning to prepare and intercede on behalf of people before destruction comes. God reveals to us what is going to happen long before it happens so we can intercede on his behalf. Amos 3:7 says, *"Surely the Lord God will do nothing, but he reveals his secret unto his servants the prophets."* KJV

I can truly say we are at a time when the manifold wisdom of God will be revealed through the Church. The church of Jesus Christ is standing and resisting the devil's plans in prayers and fasting and declaring the word victory by faith over the nations. God kept the church on earth for such a time as this. With faith the church quenches the fiery darts of the enemy. God has made the church more than conquerors and victorious. Jesus is the only hope of the world and He rises in His church.

The Church can only be effective in stopping the devil when her obedience to God is complete. That is the imagination in the Church's heart has to be filled with the righteousness of God. The weapons of our warfare to fight the devil are only mighty through our obedience. The Church that obeys God is the most powerful and invincible force on earth.

For though we walk according to the flesh, we do not war according to the flesh. For the weapons of our warfare are not carnal but mighty in God for pulling down strongholds, casting down arguments and very high thing that exalts itself against the knowledge of God, bringing every thought into captivity to the obedience of Christ, and being ready to punish all disobedience when your obedience is fulfilled. 2 Corinthians 10:3-6 NKJV

To the intent that now the manifold wisdom of Gold might be made known by the church to the principalities and powers in the heavenly places, according to the eternal purpose which He accomplished in Christ Jesus our Lord. Ephesians 3:10-11 NKJV

Darkness has risen over the world.World governments are using the disease to silence the church knowing fully that only the Church has the authority on earth to stop them. The Church is here to enforce the will of God. Darkness is rising over the nation. God forbids that the Church will be silenced.

When darkness rises over the nations, the Church will shine its light. As long as the church is on earth, she is the light of the world. People are to run into the church and experience the saving power of Jesus. The glory of the Lord is rising over the church and taking over the world.

Its interesting to note that the Church is going to become more in charge when the darkness covers the world. It's at this point that the glory of God will rise over the Church in power. That way God will draw the world to the church. The Church that obeys God is the Ark that will preserve humanity from the wickedness the devil is unleashing.

The Church that imagines righteousness and obeys God becomes the light of the world. Jesus is in the midst of the people who obey Him.

"Arise, shine; for your light has come! And the glory of the Lord is risen upon you. For behold, the darkness shall cover the earth, deep darkness the people; but the Lord will arise over you, and His glory will be seen upon you. The Gentiles shall come to your light, and kings to the brightness of your rising. Isaiah 60:1-2

"As long as I am in the world, I am the light of the world." John 9:5

Nothing catches God by surprise because He knows the intent of the heart of men. He knows about things before they happen. The devil can never catch God unawares. Everything is naked before Him. And God prepared people who are sensitive to him to His leading and are willing to obey Him.

We are living in days that are similar to the days of Noah. I can only imagined God's Heart when He looks from His Throne room.

"For the eyes of the Lord run to and fro throughout the whole earth, to show Himself strong on behalf of those whose heart is loyal to Him. In this you have done foolishly; therefore from now on you shall have wars." 2 Chronicles 16:9 KJV

Men create idealism to push God out of the heart of men in order to subject the world including the church to their rule. The power of the Church is in standing in obedience to God and not to any man. When the church submits to God, God will lift her up so the Church will be able to resist the devil in faith.When the Church does that the devil will flee.

The Church will not give in to obey man but God. When the Church obeys God, God makes her the hope of humanity. The Lord in the midst of His Church is might and Christ in the Church is the hope of glory.

Be sober, be vigilant; because your adversary the devil walks about like a roaring lion, seeking whom he may devour. Resist him, steadfast in faith knowing that the same sufferings are experienced by your brotherhood in the world. 1 Peter 5:8-9 NKJV

The Lord your God in your midst,
The Mighty One, will save;
He will rejoice over you with gladness,
He will quiet you with His love
He will rejoice over you with singing.
Zephaniah 3:17 NKJV

God directed me to write this book so that people will know the evil the devil is bringing to the world and how they can stop him. That he will try to control the church, but when the church resist him stedfast in faith and obey God, Jesus gets manifested to destroy the works of the devil. Covid19 is one such work of the devil and there will be more. It is our responsibility to manifest Jesus through our obedience so He can destroy the words of the devil (1 John 3:8).

Mighty Move of God

When God moves, miracles happen and revival are birth. That is why God is looking for people whose heart are right towards Him to move on their behalf. That way He brings revival to the earth as He did during the time of Noah.

What is happening today is no different from what happened in the days of Noah. The devil has taken captive the soul of men to do His will. Wickedness has escalated to a proportion that is hard to define. This means the devil doesn't have new tricks. He continually repeats them.

Despite all that was happening during the days of Noah, God used Noah to start a great move that swept wickedness our of the earth. My question is that is whether the imaginations of our hearts are right for God to use us to usher in His move on earth?

Everything that is happening today is only bringing to pass the days of the Lord. When God moves, miracles happen and revival are birth. God only requires people who are obedient to Him to move. When we obey God we manifest Jesus.

But as the days of Noah were, so also will the coming of the Son of Man be. For as in the days before the flood, they were eating and drinking, marrying and giving in marriage, until the day that Noah entered the ark, and did not know until the flood came and took them all away, so also will be the coming of the Son of Man." Matthew 24:37-39 NKJV

Romans 1:29-31 says, "Being filled with all unrighteousness, fornication, wickedness, covetousness, maliciousness, full of envy, murder, debate, deceit, malignity, whispers, backbiters, haters of God, despiteful, liar, deceiving, proud, boasters, inventors, of evil things, disobedient to parents, without understanding covenant breakers, without natural affection, implacable, unmerciful." KJV

Only God knows the sins and transgression and the wickedness that were committed back then during the days of Noah. If its anything like what we are experiencing now in the world, we are on the verge of mighty move of God but in a different dimension and bigger too because the world has grown.

And God saw that the wickedness of man was great in the earth, and that every imagination of the thoughts of his heart was only wicked continually. Genesis 6:5 KJV

The wickedness of man displeased God and moved Him heart to regret ever creating man. When darkness or wickedness is more on earth, God moves in a new dimension to reveal His glory.

This decision and the conclusion He arrived at then was to destroy man and start over. God's plan was to flood the earth. But then He found Noah who was a righteous through whom He preserved humanity and the species. I can assure you today God has a plan. He has a plan to save humanity.

So the Lord said, "I will destroy man whom I have created from the face of the earth, both man and beast, creeping thing and birds of the air, for I am sorry that I have made them." Genesis 6:7 KJV

We need to pray like the sons of Isaachar to understand the times and season, are in so that we can do exactly the things that God wants us to do. In asking God for wisdom to navigate the times we need to first understand it.

We can only hope today because we study the word of God and His desire for us is to obey and do His will. Isaiah 1:19 says, "If we are willing and obedient, we will eat the fruit of the land." KJV. Yes, if we obey Him will live above the wickedness, but if not we will be affected by it.

God created all of us to only obey what has taken root in our heart. Jesus obeyed God fully, because He loved God with all of His mind, heart, soul and body. This is an example that was put for us as Christian and believers to live by.

Jesus said to him, "You shall love the Lord your God with all your heart, with all your soul; and with all your mind." Matthew 22:37 NKJV

Here the Lord said I saw the wickedness of their doing and their evil hearts came up before me. Genesis 6:5 KJV

The key word in this scripture was God saw with His eyes. Saw is seen. Saw in Hebrew is ra'ah.Our God can see everything that we do in the earth. The Bible declaredHis name as the God who SEES me. EL Roi Hebrew - Ro'iy in the original Hebrew can be translated as *shepherd*, or as *seeing*, *looking*, or *gazing*.

The Bible says in 2 Chronicles 16:9 (KJV),"For the eyes of the LORD run to fro throughout out the whole earth, to shew himself strong in the behalf of them whose heart is perfect toward him. Herein thou hast done foolishly therefore from henceforth thou shalt have wars." When God moves, revival happens.

What God Requires In This Time

If you find it hard to obey the will of the Father then it will show in your life that you have not submitted to Him as Lord in your life. Whoever you obey, you are a slave to. We obey God because our hearts are filled with His love and compassion each day to do the will of the Father.

Today, many confess to be holy and righteous but do not know what God requires of them. We as believers don't know the price of the oil of salvation that the Son of man paid for each individual life, when Jesus Christ hung upon the cross for our sins and the sins of the world. He obeyed God to the shedding of His blood and death. His obedience made God raised Him from the dead.

Can you imagine how God is looking upon the world today?Can God find one righteousness person to pour into and give instruction, direction and favor, His blessing to show forth His praises? Will He find you willing and obedient?

Many have become reprobate because of the imaginations of their heart. They have hardened their hearts and have refused to listen and obey His will for their life. We are told not to harden our hearts when we hear the voice of God.

Whatever, we imagine will determine the state of our heart. It is not what we eat that defiles and disqualifies us from being chosen and used by God; it is what we allow into our heart. We must imagine the will of God to be qualified to be use by Him.

"The heart is deceitful above all things, and desperately wicked; who can know it? I, the Lord, search the heart, I test the mind, even to give every man according to his ways, according to the fruit of his doings." Jeremiah 17:9-10 NKJV

Therefore, as the Holy Spirit says:
"Today, if you will hear His voice,
Do not harden your hearts as in the rebellion,
In the day of trial in the wilderness,
Where your fathers tested Me,
And saw My works forty years.
Therefore I was angry with that generation,
And said, "They always go astray in their heart,
And they have not known My ways,'
So I swore in My wrath,
'They shall not enter My rest.'"
Hebrew 3:7-11 NKJV

GOD REPENTED that He made man. This reveals how God felt in His heart as a result of what people were doing in the days of Noah. We can understand now that our creator and maker has a heart as well emotion. He has feelings and does react to what we do against His word and will.

What was so amazing about the story is that God only mentioned to Noah what He was about to do. God mentioned certain names only when others are in involved. I truly believe when we focus our heart and eyes upon Jesus Christ and walk in obedience, we will see the glory of God revealed in our lives.

God Eyes is Upon the Righteous

For the eyes of the Lord run to and fro throughout the whole earth, to shew himself strong in the behalf of them whose heart is perfect toward him. Herein thou hast done foolishly therefore from henceforth thou shalt have wars. 2 Chronicles 16:9 KJV

Behold, the eyes of the LORD is upon them that fear him, upon them that hope in his mercy; Psalms 33:18 KJV

What happened back then in the days of Noah is repeating itself today in our generation. Wickedness and evil is on the increase. But we have Jesus Christ as our mediator who has gone before us and is interceding for us before God. God only found grace in one human being in the days of Noah, now all men have found God's grace through Jesus Christ.

Jeremiah 17: 9,10 (KJV) says "The heart is deceitful above all things and desperately wicked; who can know it? I, the Lord search the heart, I try reins even to give every man according to his ways, and according to the fruit of his doing."

Which we know that in the book of Genesis chapter 1 and 2, God created the heaven and earth in 6 days and rested on the seventh (7) day. This commandment that was spoken as an act of God's Order. Seven (7) is a completion of final establishment.

Genesis 9:1 says, Then God blessed Noah and sons and said to them, 'Be fruitful and multiply and filled (Replenish) the earth. God made covenant with Noah and his sons."

God gave them task. The blessing was bestowed on Noah.

Covenant is an agreement between two or more people. It comes with a promise from God and a part for man to play to get the promise. Biblically, God promised the children of Israel to protect them if they keep His law and were faithful unto him. God will only perform His promises, which are yeah and amen in Christ, when we fulfill our part by obeying Him.

Elisabeth Elliot said, "*Holiness has never been the driving force of the majority, It's however, mandatory for anyone who wants to enter the Kingdom.*" God commanded Noah to be fruitful and proper after the flood had ended. The righteousness of Noah was the reason why He was chosen.

Noah's obedience to God was accounted to him as righteousness. The key to the covenant God made with humanity was Noah's obedience. Also, the covenant God has with the world is based on the obedience of Jesus Christ. This committed God to making sure that He never destroys mankind but instead save them.

The key to this covenant was the righteousness of God on Noah's life, and it brought forth the divine covenant of grace to be willing to listen and trust God in the future and it please God.

God by Himself made covenant with Noah because of Noah's heart towards God. In the New Testament, God chose us based on His righteousness not ours. When we believe in Him, we become a new creature; the righteousness of God. Our faith in God makes us His righteousness.

And be found in Him, not having my own righteousness, which is from the law, but that which is through faith in Christ, the righteousness which is from God by faith. Philippians 3:9 NKJV

Jesus answered and said unto him, If a man Love me he will keep my words: and my Father will love him, and He will come unto him, and make Our abode with him. John 14:23 KJV

God's plans are revealed progressively after each obedience. I believe Noah never knew the plans God had after the flood. God's plan to bless him was there from the very beginning but was dependent on Noah's obedience to the voice of God. It was only revealed after His obedience was complete.

If we refuse to obey the smallest instruction from God, we forfeit His plans. Those little instructions that we may despise are actually key to getting into the plans of God. As we obey His voice, He reveals His plans to us. Each act of obedience leads to a bigger plan of God. Plans build on each other as we keep obeying His voice.

When we obey God, He reveals His plans to us so we can do His will. He doesn't show us all that He wants to do at once but after each act of obedience. The more we obey Him, the closer we get to His heart. Obedience is the only way to prove that we love God.

The only way we are going to be victorious in these challenging and perilous times is to hear the voice of God and obey it. This is the key to victory.

CHAPTER TWO

Instruction in My Assignment

God wants us to walk in the path of righteousness. That is the path that leads to His heart and will. To get there, we need to follow His instructions. Miracles happen when people follow the instructions of God. God's instructions are to guide into the center of His will for our lives.

At the wedding in Canaan, Jesus first miracle happened when people followed His instructions. His mother instructed the people to obey whatever instructions He gave them. And when they did as He instructed them, water was turned into wine. It happened to be the best wine.

Do what God instructed you to do first, then miracle will happen.

John 2:1-5 says, And at the marriage wedding they had ran out of wine and the mother of Jesus said to him, "They have no wine." Jesus said unto her, "Women what does your concern have to do with me? My hour has not yet come" His mother said unto the servant, "whatever he say do it."

Trust in the Lord with all your heart, and lean not on your own understanding; inn all your ways acknowledge Him, and He shall direct your paths. Proverbs 3:5-6

Your miracle is always in your obedience of God's instruction. If you will not obey God's instructions, you will not have His miracles and blessings. He will direct your steps on the right way to go.

Any time God give you instruction it will create miracles and deliverance and victory in your life.

Two years into my marriage, I was unable to conceive. I never used birth control pills. I visited my mother one day and met a prophet who was visiting. He prophesied to me saying, "I see a baby coming; a baby girl coming out of your womb." I felt lead to sow a seed of faith. I obeyed as I was instructed. A month after that, I was pregnant. But that wasn't the end.

While pregnant, I started to bleed. I was rushed to the hospital and the doctor said, "If you don't stop bleeding, you will lose child. So I called my mother and she prayed. In her prayer, she reminded God of His word and what the prophet had spoken, and she also said, "Lord, you told Sharon to sow a seed toward the word that was spoken to her."

So the doctor came back into the room and said, "If you haven't stop bleeding in an hour, we will do a D&C." After an hour, I stopped bleeding. I heard the Lord say, "Believe in the prophet." 2 Chronicle 20:20. I gave birth to 6 pound 6 ounce healthy baby girl.

God always gives us instruction and direction for our life. It's up to us to choose either to obey God or not.

The best way to live a great life is to always be open to listen to instruction from God. That is the best way to achieve greatness in life.

Keep hold of instruction; do not let go, guard her, for she is life. Instruction is the highway of life; the life of God. Proverbs 4:13 NKJV

Exodus 24:12 (NKJV) says, "The Lord said to Moses come up to me on the mountain and wait there, that I may give you the tablets of stone, with the law and the commandment, which I have written for their instruction."

Evil Association Corrupts Our Heart

Adam was given instructions by God. He was not to eat of the tree of knowledge of good and evil. Eve wasn't the one who received the instructions. As such she never disobeyed God by eating the fruit. Even if Adam had told her not to eat, she would have disobeyed Adam not God.

God will never hold you accountable for what you did if it's not in direct violation of the word He gave you. His instruction must be to you directly for Him to hold you accountable. That is why we all must be sensitive to the voice of the Holy Spirit.

Nothing happened after Eve ate the fruit. They only became naked after Adam ate. It's important that we always walk in obedience to the instructions that God gives us. When we disobey God's direct instructions to us, we get chased out of His blessings just as Adam and Eve were chased out of the garden of Eden.

The case of Adam simply shows that we need to be careful the kind of association we keep. Because we can be influenced to either obey God or disobey Him. Eve associated with the enemy and he influenced her. She associated with her husband, Adam, and influenced him to disobey God. Evil association will always corrupt good and righteous behavior.

When you associate with those who obey the voice of God, they will certainly influence you to be obedient to God. However, if you associate with the disobedient, you will certainly be influenced to be disobedient to God.

Blessed is the man who walks not in the counsel of the ungodly; nor stands in the path of sinners; nor sits in the sear of the scornful; but his delight is in the law of the Lord, and in His law he meditates day and night. Psalm 1:1-2

Then to Adam He said, "because you have heeded the voice of your wife, and have eaten from the tree of which I commanded you, saying, "You shall not eat of it':

Cursed is the ground for your sake;
In toil you shall eat of it
All the days of your life.

Then the Lord God said, "Behold, the man has become like one of Us, to know goops and evil. And now, lest he put out his hand and take also of the tree of life, and eat, and live forever"- therefore the Lord God sent him out of the garden of Eden to till the ground from which he was taken. So He drove out the man; and He placed cherubim at the east of the garden of Eden, and a flaming sword which turned every way, to guard the way to the tree of life.
Genesis 3:17, 22-24 NKJV

My write, Dimeji, shared his experience with me. When he got to the city God directed him to go to, he associated with church folks who were walking clearly in disobedience to God. They were pastors but only in title. Before he got to the city, God had told him what to do. God had told him to tithe to a certain man of God. The people he associated with were against tithing so they influenced him against it. he ended up not obeying God.

As a result, he never heard the voice or instruction of God for next three years. Within these three years, he experienced the curse. Nothing worked for him. He worked and earned money but can't account for what he did with the money. One of his shoes got spoilt and he had to use needle to put it together. Poverty became his friend.

At the end of the three years, he asked God for forgiveness and consecrated himself to do what God had instructed him to do. When he did it, God blessed him with so much money at once. It was like all that God had held back over the 3 years got released to him at once.It was his season of restoration.. He was overwhelmed by the blessings of God.

When God gives you instructions, there is nothing hard about obeying the instructions. The more you obey His instructions, the more you get deeper into His will, purpose and experience His blessings. Avoid people who are walking in disobedience so you won't be influenced to be disobedient.

Obedience Places Blessings On Your Children

When I looked at my life and the blessing upon me and my family, I can see that God has blessed me as a result of the obedience of my grandmother and mother. God promised to bless our generation when we are obedient to Him.

God can make a covenant with your children, their children, their grandchildren and great grandchildren if you will make the decision to obey all His instructions to you.

"Therefore know that the Lord your God, He is God, the faithful God who keeps covenant and mercy for a thousand generations with those who love Him and keep His commandments, and He repays those who hate Him to their face, to destroy them. He will not be slack with him who hates Him; He will repay to his face. Therefore you shall keep the commandment, the statues, and the judgments which I command you today, to observe them." Deuteronomy 7:9-11 NKJV

This reminds me of the story of Jehu and how he did the right thing in the sight of God and God blessed His generation. This is really amazing. If we walk in disobedience, we are not only doing that to ourselves but also our generations. We activate the curse in our generation.

Can you imagine that what you are going through today may just be as a result of the disobedience of your grandparents or parents? This will help you have a better perspective whenever you think of disobeying the instructions of God.

If you obey God, your generation gets blessed. If not, they will receive the curse. As for me and my house, we have entered a covenant to always obey God. My grandmother and mother left an example for us to follow in obeying God.

And the Lord said to Jehu, "because you have done well in doing what is right in My sight, and have done to the house of Ahab all that was in My heart, your sons shall sit on the throne of Israel to the fourth generation." 2 Kings 10:30 NKJV

Jehu reigned over Israel for a total of twenty-eight years. God always grant success and blessings to people who obey Him. We all need to learn from Jehu and make sure that whatever God instructs us to do, we do.

You have to continue to obey God if you want to see the blessings of God flow down through your generations. The instructions of God when obeyed always manifest His blessings in one's life and generations.

Instruction is A Guide To Life

God gave the children of Israel a life time instruction that will guide them and give them direction and commandment to live by. A journey that would have taken them forty days if they had obeyed God, took them forty years as a result of disobedience.

You may be suffering delays in your life right now because the devil is hindering God's blessing or you may be thinking that God isn't faithful (God is always faithful), but it may be as a result of your refusal to obey the instructions God had given you. Disobedience cause delays in our blessings. However, when you follow God's instructions, the blessing will come upon you and overtake you with speed.

The fear of the Lord is the beginning of Knowledge: but fools despise wisdom and instruction. Proverbs 1:7 KJV

Hear, ye children, the instruction of a father, and attend to know understanding. Proverbs 4:1 KJV

He is in the way of life that keepeth instruction: but he that refuseth reproof erreth. Proverbs 10:17 KJV

Apply thine heart unto instruction, and thine ears to the word of knowledge. Proverbs 23:12 KJV

The fear of God makes us to treasure and reverence every instruction that comes from God. Those who fear God never take His instructions for granted. They know it's the only way to the pathway of abundance and greatness in God.

What Jesus is saying today is that we must follow the rules and instructions of God and keep His commandment. The will of God, the very essence of God's divinity and divine power is activated in our lives when we obey and listen to his voice.

Receiving instructions from the mouth of God is like a feeling of fresh water pouring out of a fountain to give life into a garden that needs water to survive. It takes God's instruction to guide us and keep us on the path of righteousness. It's like a windfall of love.

When God gives you instructions, think it with your mind and believe it with your heart. God sees and knows your desires.

Job 22:22 (KJV) says, "Receive, please, instruction from His mouth and lay up His words in your heart. If you return to the Almighty, you will be built up; you will remove iniquity far from your tents. Then you will last your gold in the dust, and the gold of Ophir among the stones of the brooks. Yes, the Almighty will be your gold and your precious silver." Job 22:22-25 NKJV

If we follow the instruction of God, He becomes our inheritance and treasure.

Fear Stops Our Obedience

People see me as a woman of faith and obedience and that is true. But I have also had my own share of fear as Peter had. In Matthew 14:28-33,

Peter saw Jesus walking on water and asked that Jesus bid him to come. Jesus then said, "Come." And Peter acted on the word in obedience and as a result he started to also walk on water like Jesus.

This teaches me that when we walk in obedience to the voice of the Lord, miracles happen and we are able to do exactly what the Lord does. It is the key to commanding the supernatural.

But then something happened when Peter took His eyes off the word and started looking at the circumstance around him. That was when he began to sink. He had to call on the Lord to save him. He doubted the Lord. He became afraid.

Peter moved from the spiritual to carnal. It's way easy to move from spiritual to carnal than to move from carnal to spiritual. We can only please God when we are spiritual, that is our hearts and minds are set to obey God.

For those who live according to the flesh set their minds on the things of the flesh, but those who like according to the Spirit, the things of the Spirit. For to be carnally minded is death, but to be spiritually minded is life and peace. Because the carnal mind is enmity against God; for it is not subject to the law of God, nor indeed can be. So then, those who are in the flesh cannot please God. Romans 8:5-9 NJKV

This reminds me of something that happened when I was invited to speak at the funeral of a young girl. As I stood before the casket ministering, I looked at the baby and noticed that her eyes were opened. She opened her eyes twice and looked at me. After the funeral I went and asked her parents whether they saw her open her eyes and they told me its because children are not embalmed before burial.

But I knew that I saw her eyes opened. Now I understood that it was God who opened my eyes in the spirit to see what He wanted to do. All He wanted me to do was to speak what He showed me and He would have raised that little girl. I didn't speak because I was afraid: afraid of what people will think of me and say if the girl didn't rise up. So because of fear, I disobeyed God. Fear is really a snare.

It's painful to me now. I had the power to raise her up but fear didn't allow me to. Like Peter, I focused on the circumstance around me and not what the Lord showed me. Jesus said He only did what God showed Him to do. If He didn't see the Father do it, He won't even dare. But I saw into the spirit realm and saw God opened her eyes.

Then Jesus answered and said to them, "Most assuredly, I say to you, the Son can do nothing of Himself, but what He sees the Father do, for whatever He does, the Son also does in like manner. For the Father loves the Son, and shows Him all things that He Himself does; and He will show Him greater works than these, that you may marvel. For as they Father raises the dead and gives life to them, even so the Son gives life to whom He will. Most assuredly, I say to you, the hour is coming, and now is, when the dead will hear the voice of the Son of God; and those who hear will live. For as the Father has life in Himself, so He has granted the Son to have life in Himself, and has given Him authority to execute judgment also, because He is the Son of Man. John 5:19-21, 25-27 NKJV

I saw God raised her up. I am the Son of God and also the Son of Man. I have authority in heaven and on earth. God and the hosts of heaven waited for me to speak the word and say what I saw with faith, but I feared. My words would have called forth the things that be not as though they already existed. We see and then we speak. That way we engage God to act.

Fear has made many of us not to obey God. We have not been given the spirit of fear but of power, love and a sound mind. If we really love the Lord, we won't entertain fear because perfect love cast out fear.

We have to fix our eyes on God and stay spiritual to obey Him if we are to follow His instructions. Don't fear, whatever God shows you in the spirit, say it for everyone to hear. That commits God to make it a reality.

Restart and Finish

We, as the body of believers, have been given the greatest gift on planet earth and the opportunity to live and share the love of Jesus Christ and to have a relationship and fellowship with our Heavenly Father.

We are to be the expression of God's love to humanity. We spread the fragrance of God when we obey His instructions. We cannot love anyone except we first love God. We demonstrate our love for God and people by obeying God.

That was exactly what Jesus did. He demonstrated His love for God and humanity by dying one the cross of calvary.

But God demonstrates His own love toward us, in that while we were still sinners, Christ died for us. Romans 5:8

For this is the love of God, that we keep His commandments. and His commandments are not burdensome. 1 John 5:3

Nothing reveals God's heart to us like following His instructions. Follow God's instruction today it will bring you the crown of life, and make you victorious and more than conquerors.

The Bible says in 1 Corinthians 13:1 (KJV), Love is patient, love is kind, it does not envy it does not boast, it is not proud, It does not dishonor others, it is not self-seeking, it is not easily angered,, it keeps no record of wrongs;

Above all else guard your heart, for everything you do flows from it. You have to make sure that you guard your heart so that you can continually walk in love and live in victory. if your heart gets corrupted, you will stop obeying God. As a result, you won't be able to express the fruit of the Spirit.

Instructions Make You Wiser

There is nothing that makes us wise in life than following the instructions of God. God is wise as such His instructions can only lead us to become as wise as Him. That is why obeying the instructions of God is wisdom.

There are things I have done that seemed foolish but then when the results came out, everyone thought I was wiser. The truth is that obeying the instructions of God was what made me wise. Obedience is the best way to walk with God.

When you walk with the wise you will be wise. Following the instructions of God is walking with God. We become as wise like God when we obey His instructs. God gives us His wisdom

The key then is to make sure that we are constantly opened to receiving instructions from God. We must not do anything without first seeking instructions from God. no matter, what happens, the first thing to do is to seek God for instructions.

But seek ye the kingdom of God and His righteousness and all these things shall be added to you. Matthew 6:33 KJV

David was seen as wise because he never lost a battle. He always sought the instructions of God before he took any step. He never went to battle without an instruction from God.

You can only be victorious in life if you obey the instruction of God.

Hear instruction, and be wise, and refuse it not. Proverbs 8:33 KJV

Give instruction to a wise man, and he will be yet wiser: teach a just man, and he will increase in learning. Proverbs 9:9 KJV

And we know today that the Spirit of truth abides inside of us when we walk according to His plan and His will and in obedience to His voice.

And the Spirit of God continually instruct us in righteousness and on the way we should go. If we follow Him, we experience the fullness of God.

God wants us to keep His word and live it as righteous vessel unto the Lord's will.

If you abide in Me, and my words abide in you, you will ask what you desire, and it shall be done for you. John 15:7 NKJV

As we remain in obedience to the will of God we will become transformed into His likeness; we become a duplicate of the Most High God which is Christ through His Spirit.

Jesus was expressing that without the love of God it is impossible to obey and do the will of the Father. We must first abide in the love of Jesus Christ that's the beginning of our hope in Him. We must exercise our love by acting upon it by surrendering to the will of Father which art in Heaven.

The Bible says, "For God so Love the world, that He gave his only begotten Son, that whosoever believeth in him should not perish but have everlasting life. John 3:16 NKJV

Jesus is glorified today not because He is the Son of God but as a result of His obedience to the instructions of God. God sent Him to the earth with an instruction to follow. His major preoccupation was to make sure that His obedience to the instructions was complete. and when it became complete, God exalted Him and gave Him a name that is above all names. He became the savior of the whole world.

You too will be glorified by God when you hear and heed His instructions on how to go about what He sent you to do.

Willing To Obey

Everyone who God has blessed, has been willing to obey the instructions of God. Abraham was willing to sacrifice His one and only son, Isaac, to God in obedience. Joshua was willing to jettison his strategy to embrace that of God to take over Jericho. David was willing to obey whatever God instructed him in order to win battles. Jesus was willing to carry His cross in obedience. Are you willing to obey God?

Obeying the instructions of God may look foolish to you and others but it brings the best results. Sometimes, it really looks foolish to me. However, I have found that the foolishness of God is wiser than the greatest wisdom of men.

Because the foolishness of God's wiser, and the weakness of God is stronger than men. But God has chosen the foolish things of the world to put to shame the things which are mighty; and, the base things of the world and the things which are despised. God has chosen, and the things which are not, to bring to nothing the things that are, that no flesh should glory in His presence. 1 Corinthians 2:25, 27-29 NKJV

We become free when we obey God's instruction. It is the highest way to express our love to God. True love for God is about hearing His instruction and following it. That is the whole duty of man. Thich Nhat Hanh said, "True love has the potential to heal and transform any situation around us and bring a deep meaning to our lives Freedom,"

Let us hear the conclusion of the whole matter; Fear God, and keep his commandments: for this is the whole duty of man. Ecclesiastes 12:13

True love for God is about hearing God's instructions and following it.

CHAPTER THREE

Hearken Diligently to Obey

And it shall come to pass, If thou shalt hearken diligently unto the voice of the Lord thy God, to observed and to do all his commandments which I command thee this day, that the Lord thy God will set thee on high above all nations of the earth. Deuteronomy 28:1 KJV

The Heart of Obedience is to hear with understanding and obey God's voice and word. The Bible plainly states in the book of Deuteronomy 6:4-5 (KJV), "Hear, O Israel: The Lord our God, the Lord is one! You shall love the Lord your God with all your heart, with all your soul, and with all your strength." The Shema from the Hebrew word for "Hear" means the uniqueness as well as the unity of God's Glory.

God's desire is for us to observe a practical monotheism which is to believe He is God and only God. Beside Him there is none other God in existence. None match up to Him.

The Lord was saying Hear O Israel: meaning pay attention Israel. If we are not making progress in life, there is a place we have disobeyed God. If we obey God we make progress; if we don't, we go backward.

But this is what I commanded them, saying, 'Obey My voice, and I will be your God, and you shall be My people. And walk in all the ways that I have commanded you, that it may be well with you. Yet they did not obey or incline their ear, but followed the counsels and the dictates of their evil hearts, and went backwards and not forward.' Jeremiah 7:23-24 KJV

Obedience is far better than sacrifice. God will not accept anything, seed or sacrifices, in place of obedience. Wherever we stop obeying God, He stops blessing us. He cannot bless us even if He wants to when we are walking in disobedience.

When things are not working the way they are supposed to, we should check for any act of disobedience.

We become kings when we obey God and slaves when we disobey. Whoever we obey, we are slaves to. When we obey God, we become sons of God and kings over the earth.

Go Up And Pray

The Kingdom of God suffers violence but only the violent takes it by force. We are called to battle. We have to be very sensitive in the spirit if we want to win the war. Weapons are being formed against us, but when we obey the voice of God, those weapons will not prosper. We are to employ the force of prayer and faith to win the battles of ministry.

I have had my own share of battles in ministry. And I will say only obeying God has kept me from being consumed. But in order for us to be victorious, we have to make sure that our obedience is complete. That is to say there is no sign of disobedience in us no matter how little. When we obey God totally, then He will manifest Himself for us.

For though we walk in the flesh, we do not war according to the flesh. for the weapons of our warfare are not carnal but mighty in God for pulling down strongholds, casting down arguments and every high thing that exalts itself against the knowledge of God, bringing every thought into captivity to the obedience of Christ, and being ready to punish all disobedience when your obedience is fulfilled. 2 Corinthians 10:3-6 NKJV

He who has My commandments and keeps them, it is he who loves Me. And he who loves Me will be loved by My Father and I will love him and manifest Myself to him." John 14:21 NKJV

There is no way we are going to lose any battle if we obey God. David always inquired of the Lord before going to war. He never lost any war when He obeyed God.

In 2 Chronicles 20, the people of Moab and Ammon came against Jehoshaphat the King of Judah. He called his people to seek God. And as they sought God, He gave them a word. When they obeyed what God instructed them to do, He set ambushes against the enemies. Judah won the battle because they obeyed God's instruction.

While holding a conference, I met a leader. Through the leader I met other people who were associated with her. The leader told me that the Lord told her that I will be going on a cruise. They invited me to join them on the cruise.

On the ship, everyone had on long dresses that covered their legs, but I came with a short dress. My style was very different from theirs. We travelled from Florida to Bahamas. I never knew they were witches.

As we journeyed, God told me to start fasting. I didn't know why, but I obeyed immediately. He told me He wanted to show me something. The woman I was put in the same room with had a wrong spirit; I could sense it.

In the middle of the night, The Lord told me to go up around 3am. The lady in the room with me asked where I was going. I told her that I was going to pray. She asked if she could follow me. We went up as high as they would allow us to go on the ship. There I lifted my hands and began to pray.

I overheard the lady speaking to the security man. I was focused on appreciating and magnifying God. They had schemed against me but God was about to humble them. I heard the lady saying to the security who asked her, "Is she trying to commit suicide?" She answered that I was praying to God.

It was pitch dark because we were in the middle of the sea. The only light was on the ship. As I was praying, I heard screaming, "How did you get the hand of God to show up in the sky?" I looked and saw the hand of God in the sky. I just kept magnifying God. The lady said, "If you can get God's hands to show, who are you?"

Hearken

The price is very sure when it comes to obedience but very simple if you are ready to obey God. When God say Hearken that means to give heed or attention to what is said or being said to, listen. We are the children of God, and His desire is for us to listen to His voice and command. The Lord wants us to hear with our heart and follow His plan for our life.

I have witnessed in my life and the lives of others how we have missed much of what God is because we walk in doubt and don't believe what God is saying. The simple proof of faith is obedience to the voice of God.

There are many voices in the earth to respond to. However, how do you differentiate the voice of God from the other voices? Well for sure the word of God guides us into truth and righteousness and it also create a path of understanding and knowing what is the will of the Father for your life. This path gives life even when we don't fully understand God's ways. We have to trust Him and walk in the path through obedience to His instructions.

Just a small instruction gives us victory over our enemies.

There are times when we assume that it is the Lord's voice we heard, when in actually sense its not. There are many kinds of voices and each has its consequence. Only the voice of God when obeyed takes us into His plan for our lives.

Sometimes we can hear God's voice just as clear and other times we second guest ourselves to really be sure whether it was God speaking to us, and then we doubt if it was God speaking to us. When God speaks we must listen (hearken) to obey and not doubt it. Anyone who looks or draw back will not bring pleasure to God.

The Bible says, "Hear O, Israel; The Lord thy God the Lord is one." Deuteronomy 6:4 KJV

Diligence

It means to be steady, earnest and energetic or exertion to accomplishment, love earnestly and to choose wisely to care; heed; heedfulness. You heart comes from your heart. When you guard your heart from the world, you will be diligent in the things of God.

Above all else guard, thy heart with all diligence for out of flows the spring of life. Proverbs 4:23 KJV

Diligence is the philosopher's stone that turns everything to gold. You need to diligent hear the voice of God in order to put in the effort earnestly to obey Him.

God is saying be diligent to do your best as in 1 Peter 1:10 (KJV), Wherefore the rather, brethren, give diligence to make your calling and election sure: if ye do these things ye shall never fall in our daily life. Be persistent in doing things that God ask of us to do in the Kingdom of God, as becoming prudent students in the kingdom.

God desire for His children to be wise and to be ahead of the enemy's plans. We must become actively engaged in acquiring any type of knowledge to enhance the efforts we put into the business that we undertake and other aspect of our lives

The Bible says those who diligently seek the Lord will be rewarded with many things such as a greater presence of God in their life. By obeying the voice of God and doing His will accordingly we carry His presence everywhere we go.

We must be diligent in prayer, studying, fasting, in our daily tasks, in seeking the Kingdom and God's counsell each day and in obedience to His instructions.

Having a heart of diligence releases favor and grace upon your life to do what you are called and chosen to do.

When you are diligent, you will accomplish most if not all of the goals you set in the workplace, home, ministry, marriage relationship, family, friends and social life. Even, your mind and heart will produce healthy lifestyle and you will find yourself in a wealthy place in the spirit.

Diligence will produce true faith in your life. The Bible says a slack hand causes poverty, but the hand of the diligent makes rich Proverbs 10:4 KJV

Obedience is from the heart and not the mind. If the Love of God is not fully established in our heart, it's going to be hard to obey God and do His will.

Here are five words from the commandment of the Lord that you need to make part of your life. They are: hearken, diligent, voice, listen, observed. When you do these words in your life each day, God will place above and beyond people who don't.

Sharon Spikner

The Spirit of Obedience

Just because you accept Jesus Christ as your Lord and Savior doesn't mean you are going to obey God and pursue His will for your life. You have to acknowledge that you are a born again in Christ Jesus and have His word in your heart first.

We must go to the Father and ask of Him what His will for our lives are. However, it is much easier according to Romans 12:2 when we renew our minds with the word of God.

Then Jesus required his disciples to obey Him. He always apply His word to His Disciple. We are Disciple of Christ Jesus today, so we have to obey His word. In Matthew 16:24 (NKJV), Jesus says, "If anyone would come after Me, let him deny himself and take up his cross and follow me."

The Lord wants you to totally commit to him in everything. Your commitment to God is exemplified in your obedience. Commitment means to be willing. We have to be willing to obey God.

Isaiah 1:19-20 (NKJV) says, "If you are willing and obedient, you shall eat the good of the land; but if you refuse and rebel, you shall be devoured by the sword"; for the mouth of the Lord has spoken.

My first expression when I first got saved, and began to read the word of God, (Bible), was memorable when I came across this scripture; something inside of me shook my whole being. I truly didn't understand the willing and obedience part.

I was searching and seeking my calling in God: what is it that He is calling me to do. I knew I was called to preach the gospel of Jesus Christ. I received a lot of prophecies spoken into my life by prophets. I still had many unanswered question. I was confused. I couldn't get headway in my walk with God. There were times I was so uncertain that I felt like I wasn't saved.

I began to read the Bible more and sit with wise leadership seeking their counsel. The more I read the Bible, the more challenging life became.

Things became very hard and I was disappointed. I kept moving from one challenge to another. It was like I will never stop. I lost so much, people would turn away from me. I cried out to God: what does God want me to do in this world? What is purpose in life?

Just because you are busy doesn't mean it's from God. Sometimes, that a prophetic word is released to you doesn't mean it's the season and time for you to act upon that word. You must seek God's will for your life in that season of time. *What will you have me to do Lord*, was the cry of my heart.

The formula of obedience is God's ingredients for my life. As a young lady in the Lord accepting Jesus Christ and filled with His love and salvation and praying fervently and seeking God's face through fasting and praying regular. I was taught that faithfully going to was enough.

I thought that was the will of God. As I grow in the Lord, I got understand that the Lord require total obedience from all of us.

I had to learn that obedience flows from the heart that is submitted to God's will. One thing I had to learn is that God love me no matter how wrong I was and my sins. When I began to realized that I was chosen by God and no matter what I had done in the past God was still calling me and will use me.

The thing we all need to know is that even Jesus had to learn obedience through the things He suffered. If Jesus, the Son of God, had to learn obedience, then we too must learn it. It must mean that it's very important to God.

Sometimes we think we are obeying God when we are only following our assumptions. Ask yourself this question: am I with the right people that God has chosen? Is my geographic location where God desire me to be? Am I submissive under the right Shepherds or leadership?

Relationship and companionship is so important in the Kingdom of God. Who you listen to is very important. Association will determine whether you obey or disobey God. Build relationship with people who fear God, obey Him and do His will and chances are right that you will do the same.

Many times in my walk with God, I thought I was obeying him, little did I know that I wasn't. I made so many mistakes in my life while growing in the grace of God. Many obstacles were put in my way. There were times I thought it was God but it wasn't Him.

Failure was my second name. No matter what I tried to accomplish and everything that I tried back fired on me. And I did try a lot of things. Many doors got opened and many more got shut because of trust and betrayal. Many friendships had to be ended.

In this walk with God, I endured much pain and suffering and persecution because I didn't seek God to do His will or I thought I was doing His will. The will of God gets done through obedience. No matter how you find yourself off track or feel that God is not with you or God is not listening to you, the true victory is obedience.

You are going to find rest for your soul when you cultivate a heart that is constantly in obedience to God.

The only way to prove to God we love Him is with our heart, which bring us into obedience of His will for our life.

Now hope does not disappoint, because the love of God has been poured out in our hearts by the Holy Spirit who was given to us. Romans 5:5 KJV

The Holy Spirit teaches us all things and bring things to our remembrance It is important that we rely on the Holy Spirit for answers and direction and instruction for our life to be complete and whole in him.

Jesus said to him, "You shall love the Lord your God with all your heart, with all your soul, and with all your mind. This is the first and great commandment." Matthew 22:37 NKJV

Our heart must be filled with the love of God so we can obey Him always. We have to hearken diligently to obey God.

CHAPTER FOUR

The Lion's Heart

One of the promises of God to us is to give us a new heart. And this new heart will make us walk in His statutes. He puts His Spirit in our hearts. When the Spirit that raised Christ from the dead dwells in our hearts, our hearts get transformed. We now have the same kind of heart that Jesus and Daniel have.

This is the kind of heart that only fears God and nothing more. Daniel was clearly not afraid of anyone; he was courageous in obeying God despite the threats of the king. He served the Lord with total abandon.

When they made a law against praying to God, he went out and prayed as he used to. He wasn't afraid of what might happen to him. He had what I called the Lion's Heart. He feared God only.

The fear of the Lord is the beginning of wisdom: and the knowledge of the holy is understanding. Proverbs 9:10 KJV

When Christ dwells in our heart, we possess the lion heart. He is the lion of the tribe of Judah. We become more than conquerors and the hope of glory to many people.

Fear moves us out of the will and purpose of God for our lives. If Daniel had given in to fear, he would have been tormented. He would have been driven out of the will and purpose of God for his life. That is exactly what happens when we fear.

If we fear man, Christ has not been fully grown and dominated in us. Anyone who fears, has not so learned of Christ. If you have really learned of Christ, you will put away fear, which corrupts your heart, and be renewed in the spirit of your mind. Then you will put on the new man with a lion heart which was created according to God, in true righteousness and holiness.

You will have nothing to fear if you walk in true righteousness and holiness. It is when we have something to hide that we become afraid.

We can only fulfill our purpose if we have a lion's heart. That is what happens when the word of God has dominated and conquered our heart. Lions are not afraid of anything. If you want to have that heart, you have to fear only God.

When we fear God, we get to know and take our place in the kingdom of God. We take our place when we know and pursue our Kingdom purpose. That is what you are called to do or to accomplish on earth.

Purpose is the reason for which something exists or is done, made, used. It is the divine calling of God. God is our creator and we are made in His likeness and created for him. He created us for His family and purpose.

Knowing your purpose, who God created you to be on earth, beautifies your life. However, the kind of heart you have will determine whether you are able to move towards it.

Fear of the Lord means having a deep respect, reverence and awe for God's power and authority. When we fear God, we will never fear man. And when you fear man, you will never fear God. Fear of God and the fear of man are mutually exclusive. That means in the fear of God, there is only love and never fear.

The fear of the Lord is our major assignment. When we fear God, we will obey Him. The only proof that we fear God is when we keep His commandments or obey Him. Ecclesiastes 12:13 (NKJV) says, Let us hear the conclusion of the whole matter: Fear God, and keep his commandments: for this is the whole duty of man.

The fear of God helps us to grow and become more like God- to grow in love. When we fear God, we will walk in love towards men and never fear anything. He gives us the power, love and sound mind (1 Tim 1:7). The lion heart is never timid or cowardly.

We can only obey the person we trust. If you trust God that He will come around for you, you will obey Him. If you trust a man, that you are going to obey the instructions of the man. I chose to obey the instructions of God. I know that only God is faithful and true. He cannot lie nor change His mind. Whatever He promised is yeah and amen in Christ.

God will always try our heart to know who we trust and who we are going to obey. God really tried me to know my heart when it came to my calling into full time ministry.

Thus says the Lord:
"Cursed is the man who trusts in man
And makes flesh his strength,
Whose heart departs from the Lord.
For he shall be like a shrub in the desert,
And shall not see when good comes,
But shall inhabit the parched places in the wilderness,
In a salt land which is not inhabited.
Blessed is the man who trust in the Lord,
And whose hope is the Lord.
For he shall be like a tree planted by the waters,
Which spreads out its root by the river,
And will not fear when heat comes;
But its leaf will be green,

And will not be anxious in the year of drought,
Now will cease from yielding fruit.
The heart is deceitful above all things,
And desperately wicked;
Who can know it?
I, the Lord, search the heart
I test the mind,
Even to give every man according to his ways,
According to the fruit of his doings."
Jeremiah 17:5-10 NKJV

In my early thirties, I made it a norm to go out looking for a job. But when I get a job, God always have a way of making sure that I lose the job. There were times when people tell me that I am not supposed to be working. That I should be in full time ministry. I question doing full time ministry because I wondered how I was going to take care of myself and my children.

So I started seeking God to know what He wants me to do. Because I wasn't sure about what I was to do, I asked the Lord that if its Him that wants me in full time ministry, He should send someone who doesn't know me or any of my family or members of my mother's church. The person should speak to me as a witness and confirmation before everyone who has doubted my call on what I should do.

I was a very young woman in ministry. As a young mother of two, not having anyone to take care of my needs, I had to be sure of what God wants me to do. If I am going full time, I will have to rely and trust God for the supply of my needs., he promised to supply all my needs according to His riches in glory by Christ Jesus. I knew also that in order to enjoy His supply I had to obey His instruction.

A white lady with 8 children came to our church. She and her husband were in ministry. My mother had invited her to come and preach. As she was preaching, she called me out to minister to me. She said, "You have been talking to the Lord about your friends who are doctors, teachers, and so on and you asked what God He wants you to do. You are to work full time for Jesus Christ. People don't understand the way God is carrying you. In the natural, a man has to work to earn a living. But you have been called and chosen by the Lord. You work full time for Him."

That was the answer I sought from the Lord. And I am grateful the answer came when people who were against me where present.

Most people said I was lazy and didn't want to work. They expected me to work. They tried to discredit me because I went against the grain; against what they know and believe. The Bible said the just shall live by faith. Faith is my work. I walk by faith. My money is my faith. As I trust God, He opened doors for me, granted me favor and met all of my needs.

I suffered in the hand of people who don't believe I was called into full time ministry. I believe God was testing my heart to know if I will trust Him or obey them. I chose to obey God and receive His bless.

Revelation of God Makes Your Heart Strong

Pursuing the purpose of God for your life is not going to be easy. It's tough. That is why you need the Lion's Heart to see it go through it. The kind of heart you have will determine whether you give up or not.

I have gone through a lot of things as I pursue my calling, but I refused to give up because God has given me the Lion's heart. He didn't give me the spirit of timidity but of power, love and a sound mind. Like Daniel, I have to go through it till the end.

How did I come about the Lion's heart? Of course, through the revelation knowledge of God. The more you know God, the more you possess this kind of heart. It's the heart of steel.

Look at Jesus. He endured the cross and the shame of it all. How was He able to do that? A Lion's heart. He refused to give up or give in. He was not afraid of what man can do to Him, but rather was afraid of what will happen if He refused to obey God and carry His cross to the end.

Jesus endured the cross because He knows God and understand His purpose. Daniel understood these too and decide to endure whatever it was just to bring glory to God.

The revelation knowledge of God comes only to those who fear Him. When God reveals Himself to you, your heart gets strengthened with might by His spirit. That strengthening in the inner man gives you the Lion Heart.

The secret of the Lord is with those who fear Him, and He show them His covenant. Psalms 25:14 NKJV

A wise man is strong, yes, a man of knowledge increases strength. Proverbs 24:5 NKJV

Having the Lion heart means that your heart is filled with Christ and the love of God. You only consider God's purpose and nothing else. When you get to the point where your heart is filled with all the fullness of God, that is when you have the Lion's Heart.

Those who fear God have revelation knowledge of God. Paul was never afraid of what men will do to him because He constantly prayed that he may know God and experience the power of His resurrection.

Ephesians 3: 16-19 says, "That He would grant you, according to the riches of His glory, to be strengthened with might through His Spirit in the inner man, that Christ may dwell in your hearts through faith; that you, being rooted and grounded in love, may be able to comprehend with all the saints what is the width and length and depth and height-to know the love of Christ which passes knowledge; that you may be filled with all the fullness of God."

Colossians 1:9-11 (NKJV) says, "For this reason we also, since the day we heard it, do no cease to pray for you, and to ask that you may be filled with the knowledge of His will in all wisdom and spiritual understanding; that you may walk worthy of the Lord, fully pleasing Him, being fruitful in every good work and increasing in the knowledge of God; strengthened with all might, according to His glorious power, for all patience and long-suffering with joy."

You need revelation knowledge of God to have the lion's heart. You get that through prayer and fasting.

Don't Defile Yourself

Daniel purposed in his heart not to defile himself because he feared God. He acted on the wisdom of God. There was a plot against Daniel. It was from the pit of hell. They goal was to stop him from fearing God and make him fear for his life.

They tried to find something inches life that is incriminating but since he was a man of character, they could find nothing. He was a faithful man.

So they decided that the best way to find something against him was to come up with a law that was against the law of God. So they influenced the king to make a law that no one should pray to God except to the king. Anyone who broke that law will be thrown into the lions den.

When Daniel heard about the law, he didn't try to demonstrate or protest before the king. He went home as always and prayed to His God, the only living God. He prayed three times that day.

What will make him do that? He should have been afraid for his life? Instead of praying loudly, he should hide so that no one will know that he was praying to God. He even made sure that he opened the window for anyone who cares to know that he was praying.

The lion heart is not afraid of what men can do. It fears what God can do. He wasn't moved by what the people planned, but was moved by His trust in the living God. He feared God more. He refused to compromise his faith with fear. Fear corrupts our fear and defiles our faith.

Daniel refused to broke God's law even though it contradicts human law. People who easily broke God's law to keep human laws don't have the heart of the lion of the tribe of Judah. Christ doesn't dwell in their heart.

As a consequence of breaking human law, Daniel was thrown into the lion's den. Everyone expected the lion to eat him up. The lion could not because Daniel possess their kind of heart. There was no fear in Daniel, only love. They saw Daniel as a someone superior to them. The angels of God encamped around him because he feared God.

Then Daniel said to the king, "O king, live forever! My God sent His angels and shut the lion's mouths, so that they have not hurt me, because I was found innocent before Him; and also, O king, I have done no wrong before you." Daniel 6:21-22 NKJV

The lion could not attack Daniel because Daniel feared the Lord. Nothing could harm anyone who fears God. Not even a scratch on Daniel's body because he believed in God.

Bow And Burn

When you kneel before God in prayer, you will never have to bow to any man in fear. This was the story of Daniel's friends (Shadrach, Meshach and Abed-Nego). Everyone was required to bow to an idol, but they have already bowed to their own God in fear. They refused to bow to the image.

When you bow to God in reverence, you will always stand to man. And stand they did stand. They stood for God while others bowed to the image. They knew the punishment for not bowing to the image.

They were told if they didn't bow, they will burn. But they knew their God that even if they were thrown into the fiery furnace, they will not burn because they know their God is trust worth.

The three Hebrew boys purposed in their heart never to fear man, so they refused to bow to graven images. They chose to bow for God. God sent His angels to protect them because they possessed a lion heart. They trusted in their God.

When you have the lion's heart, you will trust God. You know that God has your back no matter what. They trusted that even if they were thrown into the fire, their God will still protect them.

Blessed is the man who trusts in the Lord, and whose hope is the Lord, for he shall be like a tree planted by the waters, which spreads out its roots by the river and will not fear when heat comes; but its leaf will be green, and will not be anxious in the year of drought, nor will cease from yielding fruit. Jeremiah 17:7-8 NKJV

Shadrach, Meshach, and Abed-nego answered and said to the king, "O Nebuchadnezzar, we have no need to answer you in this matter. If that is the case, our God whom we serve is able to deliver us from the burning fiery furnace, and He will deliver us from your hand, O king. But if not, let it be known to you, O king, that we do not serve your gods, nor will we worship the gold image which you have set up." Daniel 3:16-18 NKJV

Their trust in God only enraged the king and he commanded the heat of the furnace be increased seven times. What the king doesn't know that those young people know is that God is a consuming fire. His fire burns more than any human fire.

At the kings command, they were bound and thrown into the fiery furnace. As they fell inside, God's presence took over the furnace. Their Lord appeared with them in the fire. They trusted Him and he showed up for them. Even the king was astonished. When they were brought out, their clothes didn't even smell of smoke.

God will always how up for you when you trust Him. He has never allowed to fall. When I act blindly, trusting Him, He has always showed up for me. At the end, I get more blessed because I trusted Him.

When you posses the lion's heart, you will have:
Wisdom (Proverbs 1:7, Psalms 111:10)
Knowledge of God (Proverbs 8:13)
Prolonged life (Proverbs 10:27)
Confidence (Proverbs 14:26)
Fountain of life (Proverbs 14:27)
Rest (Proverbs 19:23)
Angelic protection (Psalms 34:7-8)
No Want (Psalms 34:9)

If you want to fulfill God's purpose for your life, you will need to possess the lion's heart. You will have to fear and trust God. You will have to be ready to leave the familiar and go on a limb into the unfamiliar.

When you trust in the Lord with the whole of your heart, He will direct you on the way you should go. And when you obey His instructions, He will come and make His home with you. You can never fail trusting God.

CHAPTER FIVE

Spirit of Excellence

Daniel stood out in a foreign nation. That is our destiny in Christ. We are not expected to be hidden, but to stand out and be extraordinary. Whenever I think about Daniel, I pray that the Spirit of Excellence will rest upon all of us. That way people will be drawn to us and we will be able to lead them to Christ.

There is no way that Spirit will come upon you and you will not be different. Daniel was. That was because the Wisdom of God was at work within Him. There is no foolishness in God, but even what we may termed the foolishness of God is far wiser than the wisdom of men.

Imagine when a man begins to seek God for wisdom in a world that is filled with uncertainty and foolishness, the wisdom of God He has will certainly placed her high above others.

Wherever you are right now, if you can just seek God for wisdom as Daniel did, you will end up above everyone. You will stand out and people will follow to you asking you from where you got that wisdom.

As for these four children, God gave them knowledge and skill in all learning and wisdom: and Daniel had understanding in all visions and dreams. And in all matters of wisdom and understanding, that the king enquired of them he found them ten times better than all the magicians and astrologers that were in all his realm. Daniel 1:17, 20 NKJV

The wisdom of God elevated Daniel to the point where He continually served different kings. No one could have done that except someone who is operating by the wisdom of God. Even in old age, the king sought him because of the wisdom of God operating in his life.

This means that when we seek God, we will get His wisdom and people will seek us to get that wisdom. He stood out from everything because the wisdom of God was at work on him.

Then this Daniel distinguished himself above the governors and satraps, because an excellent spirit was in him, and the king gave thought to setting him over the whole realm." Daniel 6:3 NKJV

Daniel lived in the midst of all these momentous events. He was deported to Babylon as a teenager, he was a close confident of Nebuchadnezzar throughout the Babylonian king's reign (605-562 B.C). Daniel served King Cyrus, the Persian Ruler who conquered Babylon.

Prophet Daniel served under the following kings:
King Jehoiakim of Judah
Nebuchadnezzar of Babylon
Belshazzar of Babylon
Nebonidus of Babylon who is not mentioned in the book of Daniel
King Darius
King Cyrus the Great/Cyrus the Persian

He began to tell and express the sovereignty of God even over nations that was very powerful. God had chosen Israel as His own people. Many nation fought against Israel. Israel was seized and conquered by mighty nation that didn't know God.

Most of Daniel's life was spent in Babylon.

Park to $300,000 House

The word of God says that if we obey His instructions and commandments we will be blessed in everything we do. That was my story. Obeying the voice of God moved me from being homeless, sleeping at the park, to having my own beautiful house.

"Now it shall come to pass, if you diligently obey the voice of the Lord your God, to observe carefully all His commandments, which I command you today, that the Lord your God will set you high above all nations of the earth. And all these blessings shall come upon you and overtake you, because you obey the voice of the Lord your God. Blessed shall you be in the city, and blessed shall you be in the country. The Lord will command the blessing on you in your storehouses and in all to which you set your hand, and He will bless you in the land which the Lord your God is giving you. The Lord will open to you His good treasure, the heavens to give the rain to your land in its season, and to bless all the work of your hand. You shall lend to many nations, but you shall not borrow." Deuteronomy 28:1-3, 8, 12 NKJV

I was homeless. I was sleeping in the park. I had a car. One time a police officer came and told me not to sleep in the park. I was praying and asking God to direct me. He had told me not to work. So I prayed for Him to tell me what to do. One day, I had a vision and I saw a broom and mop. I asked God what that meant. He told me to go and clean new house. I was to start a business and named it, Sparkle Like A Diamond Cleaning Service.

I then drove around the neighborhood. He instructed me to clean houses that are $300,000 and above. I found a place where new houses were being built. I went in. There were many Mexicans there who were building the houses. I then ask for the builder.

I met the builder and asked him if he had anyone to clean the houses for him. He said no that he just started the business of building houses. He was looking for someone to clean the houses. He asked whether I had experience in cleaning. I told him I can learn to clean houses. We made a deal and that day I got the job.

Those houses were beautiful. The Lord told me to decree and declare what I want in my house as I cleaned the houses. So I cleaned the houses as if they were mine. I took care of everything. I asked God to help me clean a million dollar house. He opened the door and I cleaned a $1.5 million house. It has 25 rooms. I had to employ people to help me clean it. God blessed me two-fold: I was paid for my work and at times I slept in those house since I have the key. I charge $600 per house and God provided me and my children with shelter.

From living in parks to cleaning the houses, and with no direction, to owning my house, God did bless me. God opened doors and granted me favor. I am blessed because I obeyed His voice.

How Daniel Got An Excellent Spirit

He didn't get the Excellent spirit because of what he did but because of who he became. You can do all that you want, if you have not become a God seeker, God's excellent spirit will be far from you.

The excellent spirit is the Holy Spirit at work in a believer producing the wisdom and knowledge of God. There was time when the king was confused with no one to give him direction, he had to send for Daniel who had the Holy Spirit, to explain to him what he was going through.

The spirit of God will manifest the wisdom of God and understanding of mysteries to you so that people will seek you out.

There is a man in your kingdom in whom is the Spirit of the Holy God. And in the days of your father, light and understanding and wisdom, like the wisdom off the gods, were found in him; and King Nebuchadnezzar your father the king- made him chief of the magicians, astrologers, Chaldeans, and soothsayers. Inasmuch as an excellent spirit, knowledge, understanding, interpreting dreams, solving riddles and explaining enigmas were found in this Daniel, whom the king named Belteshazzar, now let Daniel be called, and he will give the interpretation." Daniel 5:11-12 NKJV

What are the qualities in Daniel that made him have the excellent spirit? They are.

Daniel was man of Purpose Danial 1:8

Everything he did was in alignment with the purpose of God for his life. He purposed not to defiled himself with the king's food because he knows that it will affect him fulfilling God's purpose for his life. You will have the spirit of excellence when you allow the purpose of God to guide you in life.

2. Daniel Was a Man of Who Feared God Dan 6:20-23; 1:20

No one can have an excellent spirit who doesn't fear God. That is because the fear of the Lord is the beginning of wisdom. Daniel was a man of integrity because he feared God. The fear of the Lord made him have the wisdom of God and understanding of spiritual things. He had so much depth in the things of God than many prophets. He God revealed the secret things of heaven and the future of the kingdom to Him. When you fear God, you become a friend of God.

3. Daniel was a man of Character Daniel 2:48

Daniel's words were his bond. He was a man of character. He wasn't a hypocrite. Whatever he says that is what he does and stand for. He doesn't say what he doesn't mean. His words and actions are aligned. There is no shadow of turning about him. He has integrity. If you are not a man of character, you will never have the excellent spirit working in your life.

4. Daniel was a man of Prayer Daniel 6:10

Daniel doesn't pray when he feels like; he has time scheduled to pray. He is a man of prayer. When the king gave out a task for people to tell him his dream, Daniel didn't try to discuss it with anyone. Instead he went to God in prayer. He inquired of God. Because he knows that there is a God in heaven who knows all secrets and is ready to reveal them. We can only connect to God's excellence spirit through prayer.

Seeking God's Wisdom Via Fast

After I studied the life of Daniel, I decided to model his life of fasting. I hold a regular fasting called the Daniel Fast. There is nothing I want in life that pertains to my purpose that God has not revealed to me when I undertake this fast. When we seek God, He cause us to prosper in whatever we do.

Daniel had a covenant with God. The terms of the covenant was for him to regular seek God for wisdom. When you ask God for wisdom, He will not withhold it from you. He will give it to you abundantly.

King David never lost a war because he was always seeking God for wisdom. God is looking for people who will seek Him so He can show Himself mighty on their behalf. God did showed Himself mighty on behalf of Daniel. He lived victoriously and prosperously in a foreign land.

No matter what you are going through where you are, if you will make seeking God a part of your life like Daniel did, you will come out victorious rejoicing. God has worked a lot of deliverance in my life as I sought Him through a fast.

When you make a covenant to seek God with the whole of your heart as I have done, you will find God and all that He has.

"…The Lord is with you while you are with Him. If you seek Him, He will be found by you; but if you forsake Him, He will forsake you." Then they entered into a covenant to seek the Lord God of their fathers with all their heart and with all their soul; And all Judah rejoiced at the oath, for they had sworn with all their heart and sought Him with all their soul; and He was found by them, and the Lord gave them rest all around. 2 Chronicles 15:2, 12, 15 NKJV

He sought God in the days of Zechariah, who had understanding in the visions of God; as long as he sought the Lord, God made him prosper. 2 Chronicles 26:5 NKJV

I made this same covenant with God. That is why I constantly go on the Daniel fast. And God always gives me the excellent spirit to operate in His wisdom, understanding and revelation of His deep things.

When we seek God, His Kingdom and righteousness through a fast, all the things that people are running after in the world will be added to us. You can join us for the Daniel Fast.

Wisdom is Obeying God

When I look back at my life and all I have gone through, I will say the wisdom of God had giving me victory. The wisdom of God is not only what you read in His word, but His voice. Obeying the voice of God and doing whatever He commands you to do is wisdom.

I have always listened to God's voice and heed whatever He told me to do. That I think is key to having the excellent spirit operating in ones life. If you are not ready to obey the voice of the Lord, you won't have the excellent spirit at work in your life.

Nothing stabilizes us from the storms of life like the wisdom of God. Jesus said in Matthew 7:24-27 (NKJV), "Therefore whoever hears these sayings of Mine, and does them, I will lien him to a wise man who built his house on the rock: and the rain descended, the floods came, and the winds blew and beat on that on that house; and it did not fall, for it was founded on the rock. But everyone who hears these sayings of Mine, and does not do them, will be like a foolish man who built his house on the sand; and the rain descended, the floods came, and the winds blew and beat on that house; and it fell. And great was lots fall."

I make it a point in my life that whatever God tells me to do that is exactly what I was going to do. It may lookalike I am foolish, but at the end of the day, I have always come out victorious and prosperous. You can never beat anyone who will hear and obey God's voice.

Benefits of The Excellent Spirit

Like Daniel, when you operate by the excellent spirit, you are going to enjoy the goodness of God. God daily loads us with benefits as we obey Him. As a result of walking in the excellent spirit, Daniel enjoyed the following:

Favor and influence with God and man

When you study the life of Daniel, you will find out that He enjoyed favor with God and man and also influence with kings. When he got promoted as a result of favor, he petitioned the king on behalf go his friends and they king also promoted them. That is favor at work. He was able to influence the king's decisions and actions.

Promotion

When you operate by the excellent spirit, you will get promoted wherever you are. The excellent spirit is both diligent and creative. Daniel got promoted each time the kings noticed the excellent spirit at work in his life. Joseph came from prison to become a prime minister of Egypt as a result of these spirit. No one who has the excellent spirit can stay under. God will bring you up and position you at the top. That is where the excellent spirit operates.

Deliverance

The excellent spirit can also stir up envy and jealousy in people who don't have it. People conspired against Daniel because of the spirit at work within. The same Spirit that raised Jesus Christ from the dead was at work in Daniel. That spirit brought him our of the trouble. That spirit was his helper. A present help in time of need. When you have the excellent spirit, you are well covered.

Revelations of the Prophetic Destiny of the Church

When you read through the revelation God gave Daniel of the kingdom of God, you will wonder how such a man in the old testament can have access to such profound revelations of God. He had the Holy Spirit at work in Him. That is the spirit of excellence. I have found myself to always have revelations of God after every Daniel fast I had undertaken. The fear of the Lord must be in my heart for me to have the secrets of the God. God confides in people who fear Him (Psalms 25:14).

It's important that in these last days that every Christian makes seeking God a habit and covenant. Like Daniel, we need to be influencing nations. We are the plan of God for the nations. We have to operate in the spirit of excellence to disciple and reconcile nations back to God.

But in order to do that, we have to operate by the Lion's Heart.

CHAPTER SIX

Surrender to God

When I turned fifteen, two things happened on the same day. My grandmother who had done great things for the Lord had just passed. I was with my mum in the kitchen. She was with friends and they were talking. I never knew my life was going to change that day.

As I sat there listening to what they were saying about my grandmother, all she had accomplished for God, the heaven opened over me and I heard the voice of God call my name three times. At first it was strange to me, but then I said yes to Him. I heard Him say, "Sharon, I am calling you to preach the gospel of Jesus Christ." It was great to get the call of God at such a young age.

My challenge wasn't the fact that God had called me that young. It was that I wasn't ready to surrender to the call. I wanted to enjoy life so I told God that he needed to suspend that calling for now and wait till I turned twenty-seven. Can you imagine? I was instructing God on what to do.

I believe I am not alone in this. You may also have resisted God and given him condition to serve him. As time went on I did the things that I wanted to do in the world and the Lord started calling me to himself, I wasn't ready to surrender to Him even at twenty-seven.He reminded me what I spoke to him at the age of fifteen. God waited on me and now it's my time to obey him and surrender to the will of Gods authority.

I may not have fully understood what it meant to surrender to God and His calling then. But as continued to grow up in faith, I got to know that it's one of the most important criteria for God to use us.

You see, I knew I was chosen to do a work for the Lord, I wasn't ready to surrender to God. Meanwhile God wanted me to surrender absolutely to His calling. There is no way I could do that when I was still alive to me. I have to first empty myself of me and then be alive to God. When God calls us, He wants our total surrender to Him.

When we get to the point where our confidence is absolutely in God, we will look only to the cross and nothing else. We must trust Him who called us that He is able to take care of us. We have to forsake everything and follow Him who called us to serve in Him.

To surrender means to cease from resisting God and to submit to His authority. It also means to give oneself up into the power of another. I wasn't that fast at surrendering to God. The angels would visit me frequently, and give me direction, at time I would be hesitated with fear and still wanted to stay out in the world. I can hear that still beautiful voice calling me to preach the gospel of Jesus Christ.

Most people struggled with surrendering to the will of God, however as they begin to learn more about God, they get to trust Him. The more you surrender to God in trust, the more you will find it easy to obey him and to do His will. It can take people long to totally give in to the call of God because they don't trust Him to take care of them. God can be trusted.

Are you like me? Have you heard the call of God on your life but are afraid to commit to God because you don't trust? From experience I want to tell you that you can trust God. He will never fail you. He is true to His word.

When you have grown up with people not keeping their words, it hard to believe and trust any person. Surprisingly, we also transpose that lack of trust to God. We think He is like every one of us. If you have issues with surrendering to God, then you need to take time to learn to trust Him.

Why was it only Peter could walk on water? He wasn't alone in the boat. Jesus said come. Anyone could have head the call and walked on water, but only Peter did that. It was simply because Peter trusted that whatever Jesus said He will back it with power. God is calling you to walk on water.

God is not a man that He should lie, nor a son of man, that He should repent. Has He said, and will He not do? Or has He spoken, and will He not make it good? Numbers 23:19 NKJV

Trust in the Lord with all your heart, and lean not on your own understanding: in all your ways acknowledge Him, and He shall direct your paths." Proverb 3:5-6 NKJV

Trusting God to keep His word is the foundation and basis of surrendering.

Is Jesus Your Lord?

God has been telling some of you to go to another city to start a ministry but then you don't want to leave the safety, comfort and security of where you are right now. But then when you get a job, you are ready to go. People who do this are serving money more than they are serving God.

If Jesus is your Lord indeed then, He is going to be the one who you are going to follow and obey. Of course, we can say Jesus is Lord by the Spirit of God. But we can only prove He is our Lord indeed if He is the Lord of everything we have.

If Jesus is not Lord of all, then He is not Lord at all. Whoever you surrender to that is who you are going to obey. I try as much as possible never to obey anything but do what God has called me to do.

Are you presently doing the will of God? If you are not doing His will, then you are not surrendered to Him. We all want to move in the power of God and do great miracles and indeed it is our heritage in Christ. However we can be doing great things for the Lord and not be surrendered to His will over our life.

I want to make sure that whatever I do is what God had told me to do. It's easy to move out of the will of God and still be doing miracles. I want Jesus to remain my Lord indeed. I want Him to continually direct my steps. I want to make sure that I seek nothing on earth but to do His will.

My body is available to do His will. Jesus is the Lord over everything I am and have. Like He told His disciples to tell the owner of the donkey He used, I want to be available for Him to work through me at anytime He so deem fit. I don't want to have an excuse not to be available.

"Not everyone who says to Me, 'Lord, Lord', shall enter the kingdom of heaven, but he who does the will of My Father in heaven. Many will say to Me in that day, 'Lord, Lord, have we not prophesied in Your name, cast out demons in Your name, and done many wonders in Your name?' And then I will declare to them, 'I never knew you; depart from Me, you who practice lawlessness." Matthew 7:21-23 NKJV

Therefore, when He came into the world, He said: "Sacrifice and offering You did not desire, but a body You have prepared for Me. In burnt offerings and sacrifices for sin You have no pleasure. Then I said, 'behold, I have come in the volume of the book it is written of Me- to do Your will, O God.'" Hebrews 10:5 NKJV

God wants His will to be done on earth as in heaven. It is our work to ensure that is done. When Jesus is our Lord, then it means we are focused to doing His will where we are.

Many of us are think we cannot do the will of God because we don't have the money to do it. If you are in this situation, money is your Lord because that is who we are obeying and not God. Doing the will of God is what produce money and not the other way around.

When God calls us, we must leave everything and trust that He has made everything ready for us to do His will. When Jesus is your Lord you will follow Him not matter what. Because you know that if you follow Him, He will make you.

Absolute Surrender

The disciples of Jesus left everything to follow Him. That is absolute surrender. My question to you is: have you left everything to follow God and do His will? If you put your hand to the plough, you should not look back. You should never have a plan B. God is not pleased with us when we turn back from following Him.

It was a decision I eventually had to make. I can proudly beat my chest and say, "I have forsaken all and followed Jesus call." And you know what He has not failed me and will never do. His word is true. If I fail, it's not because He failed but because I did. When we fail in doing the will of God, it is the because we refused to totally submit to Him

Many are in ministry today who have not left anything to follow Jesus. I don't look up to anyone but to my God. He called me and I know that He is faithful also to do all that He has promised me in His word.

If you do the will of God, you have surrendered to Him. When you are surrendered, you will love the Lord with all of your soul, heart and strength.

So he answered and said, "You shall love the Lord your God with all your heart, with all your soul, with all your strength, and with all your mind, and your neighbor as yourself." And He said to him, "You have answered right: do this and you will live." Luke 10:27-28 NKJV

When we allow the devil to posses our minds, then we are going to think His thoughts and eventually do His will rather than the will of God. Absolute surrender means for us to submit our mind, heart, mouth and body to do the will of God. Our master is whoever we submit our soul to. When we think the word of God, we are going to do the will of God.

If Jesus is your Lord, you will surrender your mind, heart, mouth and body. With your mind, you will think nothing but His word. With your heart, you will love Him only. With your mouth, you will speak His words. And with body you will do His will.

Do you not know that to whom you present yourselves as slave to obey, you are that one's slaves whom you obey, whether of sin leading to death, or of obedience leading to righteousness? Roman 6:16 NKJV

And that they may come to their senses and escape the snare of the devil, having been taken captive by him to do his will. 2 Timothy 2:26 NKJV

Whoever you obey that is who you have surrendered to. In order to surrender to God to do His will, you have to present your body to Him as living sacrifice, renew your mind with His word and have and live by the faith of the Son of God. When your mind and heart are subdued by the word of God, your body will be used to serve God. This I have found to be true in my life.

The more of the word of God I put in mind, the more of His will I get to know and do. So the secret of a totally surrendered life is one that is completely renewed by the word of God.

I beseech you therefore, brethren, by the mercies of God, that you present your bodies a living sacrifice, holy, acceptable to God, which is your reasonable service. And do not be conformed to this world, but be transformed by the renewing of your mind, that you may prove what is that good and acceptable and perfect will of God. For I say, through the grace given to me, to everyone who is among you, not to think of himself more highly than he ought to think, but to think soberly, as God has dealt to each one a measure of faith." Romans 12:1-3 NKJV

Take Up Your Cross And Follow Me

Each day I wake up, I am conscious of the fact that God has an assignment for me. I have to commit to that assignment each day and follow His instruction to do what He wants. I am to carry the cross each day and follow His leading and instruction.

Unfortunately, most Christian think that if they give their lives to Christ once, they don't need to commit to any assignment or the will of God each day. God's word is new everyday, so also does He gives us our daily bread to run the race that has been set before us.

The cross is a symbol of death as such you have to die daily to your own desires and will to submit to the will of God. If you are not crucifying your body daily, you will not be doing the will of God. Daily you have to listen for the instructions of God to do what He wants done.

Carrying the cross daily is not easy but it is required for you to achieve whatever you want to achieve. There is nothing in this life that should keep you from doing the will of God. When you die to self in Surender to God, you will come alive for God.

Then Jesus said to His disciples, "If anyone desires to come after Me, let him deny himself, and take up his cross, and follow Me. For whoever desires to save his life will lose it, but whoever loses his life for My sake will find it. For what profit is it to a man of he gains the whole world, and loses his own soul? Or what will a man give in exchange for his soul? For the Son of Man will come in the glory of His Father with His angels, and the He will reward each according to his works. Matthew 16:24-27 NKJV

Taking your cross doesn't mean enduring pain, sickness or bad spouse. It simply means dying to self. When you try to save your life in the world, you will lose it. You can only find real life and enjoy life when you submit to God and do His will.

If you are a hustler, you need to come to Jesus and take your rest. Forsake everything and cling to Him. Ask Him each morning for the word of instruction. When you follow His instructions you are taking your cross. We can only do His will when we consistently follow His instructions.

Surrender Gives Power

We can only enjoy the power and lifting of God when we submit to Him. To surrender also means to submit to His authority. We all have the desire to show off who we are and what we can do, but if we really want the power of God to be expressed in our lives, then we must submit to the authority of God.

Why do we find it hard to submit to God? It's mostly pride. We trust in our money or talent. We believe we can do anything we want, so we go on our own strength to do it. The Bible says rather than empower us, He resist us when we intentionally refuse to submit to Him.

When we refuse to submit to God's authority, our words lack the power to cause the devil to submit. In submission, we have the power to cause the devil to flee and submit to our words. That is because, when we submit to God we become one with Him.

But He gives more grace. Therefore He says: "God resists the proud, but gives grace to the humble." Therefore submit to God. Resist the devil and he will flee from you. James 4:6-7 NKJV

Surrendering to God is not just the best way to live as a Christian, it's the only way. Nothing else works. It's the life of trusting and obeying. Anyone who wants to live in the authority and blessing of God has to live continually in surrender to God.

Victory in life and ministry comes through surrendering our lives to God. I must warn you that surrendering to God will not be easy. It will be tested because it is precious to God. However you need to understand that at the end, you will be far better than if you had not submitted.

CHAPTER SEVEN

Seed of Faith

Abraham never knew that God was testing His faith. All he knew was that whatever happened, God has the ability to raise even the death. With that in mind, he took his only son Isaac to sacrifice as God had instructed him.

Many of us would have doubted as they went on the journey. But not Abraham. His eyes were fixed like a flint on making sure that God's instructions was followed. He never doubted God's word and power.

Most Christians would have argued over such an instruction. They would have doubted that God really instructed them. They may even have thought it was the devil and begin to bind the devil over such instructions.

Abraham had gotten used to hearing the voice of God. He was fully convinced that it was God's voice he heard and fully persuaded that God is able to do whatever He says.

Wasn't it God who had promised him the child in the first place? He must have reasoned. If God gave him Isaac when the womb of Sarah his wife was dead, then God should also have the ability to also raise him from the dead.

Faith is never easy. You think doing what he did was easy? No, it wasn't. It was hard. But because he believed God, he never considered anything contrary. He considered the fact but stayed on the outcome he was expected. Faith knows the outcome it desires and is unrelenting about it.

What amazes me is that Abraham walked for days to get to the place where God had instructed him to sacrifice his only son. And the child also followed his father like a lamb to the slaughter. Would you have done that?

When they got to the place of sacrifice and the father prepared the altar for the sacrifice, Isaac helped in the preparation. He even volunteered to ask his father where the lamb for the sacrifice is. And the father out of faith said, "My son, God will provide for Himself a lamb for a burnt offering." (Genesis 22:8)

What would have happened if Abraham had answered that his son was the lamb to be sacrificed? Would the child had protested or ran away? I doubt that. But one thing I know is that God would have worked with the word that Abraham spoke.

Do you know that God did exactly as Abraham had spoke? Yes, he did. Faith is the only way we can bring pleasure to God and engage Him to act on our behalf. As Abraham was about to sacrifice the son, God spoke to him.

And Abraham stretched out his hand and took the knife to slay his son.

But the angel of the Lord called to him from heaven and said, "Abraham, Abraham!"

So he said, "Here I am."

And He said, "Do not lay your hand on the lad, or do anything to him; for now I know that you fear God, since you have not withheld your son, your only son, from Me."

Then Abraham lifted his eyes and looked, and there behind him was a ram caught in thicket by its horns. So Abraham went and took the ram, and offered its up for a burnt offering instead of his son. And Abraham called the name of the place, The-Lord-WillProvide; as it is said to this day, "In the Most of the Lord it shall be provided." Genesis 22:10-14 NKJV

No one can ever get anything from God except they believe that God is able to provide for them. Everything we will ever get from God as demonstrated by Abraham will be the outcome of faith and faith only.

No one should be deceived that they will ever receive anything from God outside of faith.

Reality of The Outcome You Desire

Whatever you desire in this life is possible. As long as it is part of the promise of God, faith can make it possible. Faith confers on humans the ability and capacity of God. That is to say that whatever is possible with God is possible with anyone who has faith.

Faith doesn't just give us the want me want, it is the evidence of the things we desire to have. That is to say that even when you don't have it, faith acts like you have it.

When God changed the name of Abraham and his wife, He was teaching them how to walk in the reality of what He had promised them even when they don't really have it. Abraham became the father of nations while Sarah was the mother of nation. Here they are barren, yet their declarations was the reality they desire.

To start walking by faith, you have to know the promises of God towards you. Every scripture in the Bible is a promise of God towards you. Faith is the only spiritual force that can turn those promises into reality.

You don't need to have what God promised to behave like someone who has it. Faith empowers you to believe you have it. Nothing is impossible to faith.

Now faith is the substance of things hoped for, the evidence of things not seen. For by it the elders obtained a good testimony. But without faith it is impossible to please Him, for he who comes to God must believe that He is, and that He is a rewarder of those who diligently seek Him. Romans 11:1-2, 6 NKJV

God's people are perishing because they don't know all that God had promised them in His word. It's really liberating when you come to the knowledge of the promises of God. Knowing fully well that faith in God will make those promises a reality in your life.

Faith to obtain the promises of God will only come as you know the promises of God. The revelation of the promises of God births faith in your heart. The revelation of the promises comes when you hear and keep hearing those promises. As you meditate on them, faith is the result.

So then faith comes by hearing, and hearing by the word of God. Romans 10:17 NKJV

When faith comes, you are no longer a child but an heir. As a heir you have a right to the promises of God. They are yours.

Promise Received By Faith

We used to pray that God should do things for us but God wants us to take whatever He has promised us by faith.

If you are sick, take healing by faith
If you are poor, take prosperity by faith
If you are in need, take God's supply by faith
If you are stagnated, take God's promotion by faith
If you are barren, take fruitfulness by faith

If you are jobless, take jobs by faith
If you are homeless, take buildings by faith
If you are weak, be strong in the Lord by faith
If you want your prayers answered, use faith
If you feel defeated, take your victory by faith
If you have fallen, take your stand by faith

Whatever you can see in the word of God is yours to take by faith. You are an heir of the promises of God. When you give yourself to the promise of God in His word, it will build up your faith and cause you to inherit whatever is promised.

Abraham focused on what God told him and continually say it to himself. The word is a seed that when planted in the heart will bring forth a harvest. The Bible is a bag of seeds. You can get seeds for whatever you really want to enjoy life and have it more abundantly.

Jesus shared in the parable of the Sower how we should handle the word to produce faith in our heart. It is our responsibility to plant the word of God into our heart. The promises of God like any seed produce after it's kind.

If you sow the promise of prosperity in your heart, it will produce faith for prosperity. It's up to you to sow the promise of God. Once you have faith, you will have the promise.

But let him ask in faith, with no doubting, for he who doubts is like a wave of the sea driven and tossed by the wind. For let not that man suppose that he will receive anything from the Lord; he is a double-minded man, unstable in all his ways. James 1:6-8 NKJV

Therefore, [inheriting] the promise is the outcome of faith, in order that it might be given as an act of grace (unmerited favor), to make it stable and valid and guaranteed to all his descendants- not only to the devotees and adherents of the Law, but also to those who share the faith of Abraham, who is [thus] the father of us all. Romans 4:16 Amplified Bible

There is no way you are going to sow the promise of prosperity and have faith for healing. You should not deceive yourself because you cannot mock God. Whatever promise you sow into your heart, that is what you are going to have faith for. Nothing more, nothing less.

Be Fully Persuaded

When you give yourself whole to the promise of God that you desire to have, your progress will become evident to everyone. That was what Abraham did. He didn't just become fully convinced about God's ability. He has given himself to God.

When you operate any faith, you will never be disappointed nor put to shame. You will instead be victorious. You have to get to a point where you are fully persuaded about God.

The challenge most people have is that they don;'t trust that God has their back and is able to do whatever He says. They equate God to their human experience. God is not a man that He should lie, nor the son of man that He should change His mind. Whatever He has promised He has the ability to make it a reality.

Faith should not be based on your ability or someone you know but in God. You become fully persuaded when you know and are sure that God will not back down on His promise. His promise is sealed with His blood. His word is His bond.

Your faith should be based on who you know, your family, your job, your nation or your ability but in the living God. In Him we walk, move and have our being. Your faith must stand on the fact that God will never fail His word. No jot of His word shall fall to the ground without it prospering. Every promise of God is backed by His power.

And not being weak in faith, he did not consider his own body; already dead (since he was about a hundred years old), and the deadness of Sarah's womb. He did not waver at the promise of God through unbelief, but was strengthened in faith, giving glory to God, and being fully convinced that what He had promised He was also able to perform. Romans 4:19-21

When you get fully persuaded, you become someone with no option. You will not be in a hurry. Like Job, you will tell yourself that you are going to wait on the Lord till your change comes. When you are ready to wait forever, then it won't take long you are going to have it.

Abraham at first doubted God and looked for an option. That option became Ishmael. But after that, he became fully persuaded, he threw away every option and focus on God's promise to Him. And He did get what God promised Him.

Words of Faith Are Resources For Creation

One thing Abraham understood from the creation story was that the words of faith are the resources the Holy Spirit and the angels of God uses to make real what we believe. That was why he only spoke what God promised Him.

When God saw the earth, it was out of shape. He intended to start the creation process to put everything in order. The Holy Spirit was present and angels too. But nothing happened until God spoke the promise. This shows that Words of faith is the resource we need to present the Holy Spirit to use to create what we want.

We have to speak the work if we want the Holy Spirit to use it to make real what we want. The Holy Spirit and angels heed the voice of God's promise. We are the ones who can give voice to the promise of God.

When you believe the promise of God and speak it, you are going to have it. That is what Jesus said in Mark 11:23. Faith always speaks the word of God. The word of faith must be in your mouth for you to have it. Whatever you believe you are going to say it and have it.

By faith we understand that the worlds were framed by the word of God, so that the things which are seen were not made of things which are visible. Hebrews 11:3 NKJV

So Jesus said to them, "Because of your unbelief; for assuredly, I say to you, if you have faith as a mustard seed, you will say to this mountain, 'Move from here to there,' and it will move; and nothing will be impossible for you." Matthew 17:20 NKJV

You are going to enjoy the fruit of whatever you believe and speak. You sow the promise in your heart but harvest it by the word that you speak. You are to speak the promise of God as if it has happened.

Instead of saying I am hoping to get well, you say by His stripes I am healed. No matter how you are feeling, always speak the word of God you believe. You are imitating God as His own child.

God always speaks things that be not as though they are. You should speak what you want as if you already have it. And you are going to have it.

As it is written, I have made you the father of many nations. [He was appointed our father] in the sight of God in Whom he believed, Who gives life to the dead and speaks of the nonexistent things that [He has foretold and promised] as if they [already] existed.

[For Abraham, human reason for] hope being gone, hoped in faith that he should become the father of many nations, as he had promised, So [numberless] shall your descendants be. Romans 4:17-18 Amplified Bible

Continually call forth the things you want that God has promised you as though you already have it. Talk like someone who has it and you will have it.

Sharon Spikner

Faith Requires Work

Most people stop as speaking the promise of God. But that is not enough. Your speaking the work without the corresponding action of obedience to the voice of God will only shipwreck your faith. You have to act.

The woman with the issue of blood had faith that Jesus can heal her but then she has to act on that faith. She acted by touching the hem of His garment. She made contact and she got healed. Her actions justified her faith and she got what she was promised.

If you are waiting for the promise of God to become real in your life without taking action, you are going to wait forever without having it. That is because faith is dead without corresponding act of obedience.

But someone will say, "You have faith, and I have works." Show me your faith without your works, and I will show you my faith by my works. But do you want to know, O foolish man, that faith without works is dead? Was not Abraham our father justified by works when he offered Isaac his son on the altar? Do you see that faith was working together with his works, and by works faith was made perfect? You see then that a man is justified by works, and not by faith only. James 2: 18, 20-22, 24 KJV

Action empowers your faith. You actually show that you believe God when you take a step of faith. Peter believe that he can walk on water when Jesus told him to come, but then he had to act on that word for his faith to work. When he did, he walked on water.

Don't just speak the word of God without acting on God. The promise will show you what to do and the Holy Spirit will guide you on the way you should go. Obey the leading and your faith will be empowered to prosper in what you believe.

CHAPTER EIGHT

Obedience For the Future

I always wondered why Jesus was very effective in His assignment? What He was able to accomplish in 3 and the half years could have taken Him 60 years to accomplish or even more. He was the first person to really say I have finished my assignment.

We all are here to complete something that God has started. No one can do what God sent you to the earth to accomplish. Only you can. And there is no way you are going to achieve that without following in the footsteps of Jesus.

Jesus is our perfect example. Even though we may not attain to perfection on earth, but I believe that if we are able to follow Him, we will do exactly what He did and more. Didn't He even say that we are going to do greater works than what He has done?

Yes, He did. That is what secured leaders do. While others would have kept the secret from others, Jesus revealed it all.

What was the secret of Jesus success and accomplishment? Obedience. Every thing He did and achieved was based on obedience to the commands of His Father, our Father. If we want to succeed like Jesus, then we need to make sure that we do exactly what He did.

Following the path of obedience to the commands of God makes us one with God; unified in purpose. Jesus had only one assignment: to do the will of the Father. He never did anything that took Him away from obeying the Father.

Everywhere He went was where God wanted Him to be.
Everything He did was what God wanted Him to do.
Every word He spoke was what God wanted Him to speak.

He went, did and spoke exactly what God instructed Him to say. He enjoyed the support and backing of heaven. When you purchase a software from a company, you get to enjoy support from the company. They set up a department to support their customer.

God does likewise. When you do exactly what He instructs you to do, you will have no problem with support. The host of heaven will back you in everything that you do. You will be enjoy divine backing.

If you always do whatever God commands you to do, you will bring Him pleasure and He always back and support you.

Then Jesus answered and said to them, "Most assuredly, I say to you, the Son can do nothing of Himself, but what He sees the father do; for whatever He does, the Son also does in like manner. For the father loves the Son, and shows Him all things that He Himself does; and He will show Him greater works than these, that you may marvel. For as the father raises the dead and gives life to them, even so the Son gives life to whom He will. I can of Myself do nothing. As I hear, I judge; and My judgment is righteous, because I do not seek My own will but the will of the Father who sent Me. John 5:19-21, 30 NKJV

And He was withdrawn from them about a stone's throw, and He knelt down and prayed, saying, "Father, if it is Your will, take this cup away from Me; nevertheless not My will, but Yours, be done." Luke 22:41-42 NKJV

Therefore, when He came into the world, He said:
"Sacrifice and offering You did not desire,
But a body You have prepared for Me.
In burnt offerings and sacrifices for sin
You had no pleasure.
Then I said, 'Behold, I have come-
In the volume of the book it is written
of Me-
To do Your will, O God.'" Hebrews 10:5-7

God doesn't require sacrifices from you but your obedience. That is because when you obey His commands, you activate Him in your situation.

Disobedience Keeps You Outside His Will

Hebrews 3:18 says that God promised that those who disobeyed Him will never enter His rest. So they remained in the wilderness for 40 years. If we disobey God He will never allow us enter into His promises. We will stay outside His will. He will take care of us because He is faithful but we will never experience His best.

The more we obey God, the more we get closer to the center of his will for our lives. Many will not enter because they are disobedient. His will is for the obedient.

The children of Israel disobeyed and stay outside the promise Land until those who rebelled against God's will died. We must strive to always obey God in whatever we do. That is the only guarantee of getting into His will and blessings.

As we obey God, we get directed into the center of His will for our lives. But if we disobeyed, we get directed out of the will of God for our life. Disobedience has eternal consequences. So keep obeying God because your eternity depends on it.

Even though God promised them that He will give them the promised land, He never allowed them enter because they disobedient. Until all those who disobeyed Him died in the wilderness, He never allowed them into the promised land. If our obedience is not complete, He will never allow us enter His promises and will for our lives.

"Not everyone who says to Me, "Lord, Lord,' shall enter the kingdom of heaven, but he who does the will of My father in heaven. Many will say to Me in that day, 'Lord, Lord, have we not prophesied in Your name, cast out demons in Your name, and done many wonders in Your name?' And then I will declare to them, 'I never knew you; depart from Me, you who practice lawlessness.'" Matthew 7:21-23 NKJV

God is faithful to His promises. They are yeah and amen in Christ. But for them to become a reality, you have to obey Him. If what promised you doesn't come to pass, you must have disobeyed Him somewhere. You have to check it.

And when you realized you have disobeyed, you have to first repent of it. Then seek God to know what He will have you do. The instructions He gave you then may have been situational and may have passed. You need to seek Him to know what He will want you to do. He will start with you from a low level and build your faith till it's stronger.

He Stood By the Imagination of His Heart

My editor, Dimeji, gave me permission to reprint his story in this book. One day he was directed to watch an annual conference of a particular Bishop God has instructed him to learn from. As he listened, he heard God spoke to his heart that "you would have been one of the ministers in this program if you had not disobeyed me."

His mind immediately went back to years back when he met his wife and proposed marriage to her. God had told him not to marry her. But because he loved her and has given her his word, he went ahead to marry her. God made ways of escape for him, but he refused to heed God's instruction. He stood by the imagination of his heart. He told me that he thought he was wiser than God. He cannot make progress in ministry as he wants to because God limits him. He wished he has heed God's instructions.

Meanwhile, the wife is enjoying herself while he is not happy with himself. The truth is you should never disobey God for anyone. It's not worth it. When you are suffering they will be enjoying themselves. Always make sure the imagination of your heart propels you to constantly obey God. It's the only way to make progress. Our greatest achievements will be a fruit of our obedience to God's instructions.

He stood by his own decision, what was the imagination of his heart. As a result, he got limited in doing the will of God because he disobeyed. It stopped him from walking in the full blessings of God.

1. Christ is only Lord indeed when we obey Him
2. We can't fulfill our full potential in Christ without fully obeying God
3. We manifest the kingdom of God through Obedience
4. When we obey God we stay in His will for our lives
5. We can only operate in the kingdom of God through obedience
6. We win spiritual warfare when our obedience is complete

Hearing The Voice Of God

We can be the vessel through which God speaks to the world. We are the echo of what God says if we are submitted to Him. We can only be that if we position ourselves to hear the voice of God.

How can you obey the voice of God when you are unable to hear it. I found out that God doesn't give people a future. He doesn't ready-made a future and just deliver it into your laps.

What He does is to show you the picture of the future He wants you to have and then gives you instructions daily. Your obedience to the instructions of God builds the future for you.

We all have the ability to hear the voice of God but then only few of us really are trained to hear the voice. If you cannot differentiate the voice of God from all other voices you will hear, there is no way you are going to make any progress.

There are all kinds of voice that will speak to you and none of these voices is without consequence. These voices have significant effect on you. There voices include:

1. Voice of your flesh
2. Voice of your pain
3. Voice of your circumstance
4. Voice of your excuses
5. Voice of your insecurity
6. Voice of your fears
7. Voice of your experience
8. Voice of your mentors
9. Voice of your friends
10. Voice of your father
11. Voice of God

If you are the sheep of God you will certainly be tuned to hear the voice of God. God shepherd His flocks with His rod and voice. If you are not following His voice then you are not His sheep.

Jesus became an echo of whatever God spoke to Him. He listened to what God was saying and then say it. He only said the things that God instructed Him to say. If you are Jesus' sheep, you will hear His voice and heed it.

"He who rejects Me, and does not receive My words, has that which judges him- the word that I have spoken will judge him in the last day. For I have not spoken on My own authority; but the father who sent Me gave Me a command, what I should say and what I should speak. And I know that His command is everlasting life. Therefore, whatever I speak, just as the father has told Me, so I speak. John 12:48-50 NKJV

"My sheep hear My voice, and I know them, and they follow Me." John 10:27 NKJV

You can only hear the voice of God when His word has saturated your heart. God speaks over His multitude of His word. When His voice becomes like water in your heart, its easy to hear His voice. You can only obey the voice that you hear.

Hearing the voice of God and not obeying it is rebellion against His authority. It's better not to hear than to hear His commands and harden your heart not to obey it. The Israelites were unable to enter the promised land because they disobeyed the voice of God.

The voice of the Lord is over the waters;
The God of glory thunders;
The Lord is over many waters.
The voice of the Lord is powerful;
The voice of the Lord is full of majesty
The voice of the Lord breaks the cedars,
Yes, the Lord splinters the cedars of Lebanon.
He makes them also skip like a calf,
Lebanon and Sirion like a young wild ox.
The voice of the Lord divides the flames of fire.
The voice of the Lord shakes the wilderness;
The Lord shakes the wilderness of Kadesh
The voice of the Lord makes the deer give birth,
And strips the forest bare;
And in His temple everyone says, "Glory!"
The Lord is enthroned at the Flood,
And the Lord sits as king forever.
The Lord will give strength to His people;
The Lord will bless His people with peace. Psalm 29:3-11 NKJV

Fort the children of Israel walked forty years in the wilderness, till all the people who were men of war, who came out of Egypt, were consumed, because they did not obey the voice of the Lord- to whom the Lord swore that He would not show them the land which the Lord had sworn to their fathers that He would give us, "a land flowing with milk and honey." Joshua 5:6 NKJV

Today, if you will hear His voice, do not harden your hearts as in the rebellion." Hebrews 3:15 NKJV

Obedience doesn't help God, but instead it brings God into your affairs as a helper.

Obedience Is The Greatest Enabler

David would not have succeeded as a king in all of his battles if he had not been someone who listened to God's voice and obeyed God's instructions and commands. Those who obey God end up empowered to achieve whatever they set to achieve.

We can do nothing with eternal consequence without obeying God. That is why it's very important for us to position ourselves to obey God. All we can ever be in the kingdom and have will be based on our obedience to God's commands.

You can of your own do nothing. You can never amount to anything in the kingdom if you are not ready to obey God. Even Jesus, even though He is the Son of God, had to learn obedience by the things He suffered. He only became the savior of the world after He had obeyed God to the end.

Though He was a Son, yet He learned obedience by the things which He suffered. And having been perfected, He became the author of eternal salvation to all who obey Him. Hebrews 5:8-9 NKJV

I am today what I am because I obeyed God. If I am unable to reach where I am going, it won't be because God cannot take me there but because I refuse to obey His instructions. His instructions are the path I have to take to reach where I am supposed to go.

God knows where He wants me to be. He knows what I have to do to get there. He knows the path. So I have to wait on Him each day to receive the daily bread (instructions and commands for the day).

We can only succeed in our assignments when we submit to God instructions and keep following Him wherever He leads. His instructions will lead us to victory and triumph. We become overcomers and more than conquerors as we obey Him. We also enjoy His protection.

Now therefore, if you will indeed obey My voice and keep My covenant, then you shall be a special treasure to Me above all people; for all the earth is Mine. Exodus 19:5 NKJV

Therefore keep the words of this covenant, and do them, that you may prosper in all that you do. Deuteronomy 29:9 NKJV

This Book of the Law shall not depart from your mouth but you shall meditate in it day and night, that you may observe to do according to all that is written in it. For then you will make your way prosperous, and then have good success. Joshua 1:8 NKJV

When we obey God He enables us to be all that He has called us to be and do all that He has assigned us to achieve. Jesus was only able to say "it is finished" because He lived a life of obedience to the command of God.

He never sought His will but always seeking to do the will of God.

Sharon Spikner

Love is Obedience Not a Feeling

Many of us think that love is a feeling but it's not. It is who we are to others. It enables us to do things for people. The only proof that we love God is to obey Him.

During worship, many with tears-filled eyes always confess their love for God. Loving God is not a feeling. God is love and since we are created in His image and likeness, we are creatures of love. We are to love people as God loves them.

Anyone who says he or she loves God but doesn't obey God's command and instructions is not saying the truth. Let us not be carried away by how we feel but focus on hearing God's instructions and obeying it.

This speak more to God than just singing "I love you, Lord." The heart that obeys God's voice is the heart that is full of love for God. Obedience means you are giving your whole being to God as a sacrifice.

"If you love Me, keep My commandments." John 14:15 NKJV

"He who has My commandments and keeps them, it is he who loves Me. And he who loves Me will be loved by My Father, and I will love him and manifest Myself to him." John 14:21 NKJV

Obedience can be tough on how flesh. The instructions of God may sound foolish at times. But then when we obey Him, we should that we are giving ourselves to Him.

What is love without we giving ourselves to the person we love? You can feel love but never give yourself. What many call love is actually selfishness. When they feel good about something, they call it love. Love is not feel good, but sacrifice for others.

Love doesn't take, it gives. God loves the world and gave His best so that the world can become better. If you love God, then you will have to obey His instructions and commands.

Punish All Disobedience

God gave us authority with which we are to dominate the earth and everything He has created. We are the lords of the earth. Everything is supposed to obey us. But then when we rebelled against God, everything rebelled against us.

Disobedience to the voice of God is costly because its rebellion against His authority. When we walk in disobedience to God's instructions, everything creature on earth disobeys our authority including our body.

The things that God had created to submit to our authority and serve us begin to challenge our authority and become our lord. The waters overflow their bank in disobedience. Mosquitoes become an agent of evil rather than good. Our bodies begin to rebel and become cancerous.

Everything God has created are to obey our instructions as we obey the instructions of God. The moment we stop obeying the voice of God, we lose that authority. And humanity has gotten to a point where we are constantly disobeying the instructions of God. As a result, the earth is releasing its elements that are against humanity.

Under God's authority, heaven is the most sought after place. He placed the earth in our care so that we could make it like heaven as we obey Him. But once we start rebelling against God, we turn it into hell on earth.

Except our obedience to God is complete, we will never get to the point where everything on earth obeys and submits to our authority. The earth is under our care, our obedience would have made it like heaven but our disobedience and rebellion made it more like hell.

And being ready to punish all disobedience when your obedience is fulfilled. 2 Corinthians 10:6 NKJV

When He assigned to the sea its limit, so that the waters would not transgress His command, when He marked out the foundations of the earth. Proverbs 8:29 NKJV

As soon as they hear of me they obey me; the foreigners submit to me. The foreigners fade away, and come frightened from their hideouts. Psalm 18:44-45 NKJV

In Luke 5, Jesus instructed Peter to launch into the deep and cast the nets. Peter was a professional fisherman and he and his team had tried all through the night to catch fishes but they were not successful. He knew the best time to make a catch has passed. But in order not to look for foolish he acted in his wisdom.

Rather than nets, he decided to just use one net. Even though his obedience wasn't complete, the little act of obedience made all the fish to obey him. They came to his net and broke the net. Other fishermen had to come help him if not his boat would have sank.

He had to later apologies to Jesus for not going all out in obedience. You can only imagine the amount of fishes they would have caught that day if he had completely obeyed Jesus' instruction.

When you obey God, all that He created will also obey you. Obeying God makes you a king and lord on earth so that wherever your words are there will be power for everything created by God to submit to.

The Blessing Is Commanded

Why will obeying the commands of God turn the earth into a place like heaven? Obedience manifest the blessing of God. The Blessing of the Lord makes everything rich without adding any sorrow. It empowers every resources and created things with the ability to create wealth.

Whenever you obey God's voice, you release His blessings over your life and whatever is under your authority. God will tabernacle with you.

When the Ark of the Covenant stayed in the home of Obed Edom, it was said that God blessed his household. Imagine what happens when the God of heaven and all of His host come to stay with you? The blessing can make you live in heaven while on earth.

I bet you are getting to know how costly it is to disobey God's instructions. When you hear His voice, don't harden your heart. His instructions are always for your own good.

If you hearken diligently to obey the voice of God, you will only experience the power of His blessings. Abraham experienced that blessing and He enjoyed the lifestyle of heaven while on earth. You too can.

Jesus answered and said to him, "If anyone loves Me, he will keep My word; and My Father will love him, and We will come to him and make Our home with him." John 14:23 NKJV

But He said, "More than that, blessed are those who hear the word of God and keep it." Luke11:28 NKJV

"Now it shall come to pass, if you diligently obey the voice of the Lord your God, which I command you today, that the Lord your God will set you high above all nations of the earth. And all these blessings shall come upon you and overtake you, because you obey the voice of the Lord your God. The Lord will command blessing on you in your storehouses and in all to which you set your hand, and He will bless you in the land which the Lord your God is giving you. The Lord will open to you His good treasure, the heavens, to give the rain to your land in its season, and to bless all the work of your hand. You shall lend to many nations, but you shall not borrow. And the Lord will make you the head and not the tail; you shall be above only, and not be beneath, if you heed the commandments of the Lord your God, which I command you today, and are careful to observe them. Deuteronomy 28 :1-2, 8, 12-13 NKJV

When you obey the voice of God, you become the voice of God on earth. When you obey the voice of God, you command the blessing of God on everything under your authority.

CHAPTER NINE

Place of Favor with God

Favour means that you have the approval and backing of God. When God is favorably disposed towards us, we are favored. Like all other things God has made available for us, favor has to be received by faith.

God is not stingy with His favor as many people are. He is liberal and always goes beyond what you will ever think or ask. He exceeds our expectations in an abundant way.

I am a product of God's favor. Everything I am and I have to do can be attributed to God's favor upon my life and I am really grateful for it all. Like Abraham, I can say its God all the way and never man.

God's favor gives us the ability to do things that are humanly termed impossible. When I look at where I started this walk from and where I am now, I know that only the favor of God can make such possible.

And you know what, I am not even God's favorable child. There is no favoritism with God. We are all equal before Him. He is not a respecter of any person. He is the same towards anyone who seeks Him.

He is constantly looking for people He can favor. I hope you will position yourself to receive His favor. It will make your life sweet and your efforts sweat-less.

The Bible is filled with stories of people who enjoyed the favor of God.

Abraham enjoyed the favor of God and the king made him rich.

Isaac enjoyed the favor of God that he sowed in the land during famine and surrounded by enemies, yet he prospered and they feared him.

Jacob enjoyed the favor of God for God gave him an idea that made him richer than Laban.

Joseph enjoyed the favor of God for he was made the prime minister of Egypt.

Esther and Mordecai enjoyed the favor of God for the kind turned the decree of Haman and promoted Mordecai.

Nehemiah enjoyed the favor of God for the king gave him the support he needed to build the walls of Jerusalem.

Daniel enjoyed the favor of God for he was promoted and served successive kings.

You can also place your name among them. That is my expectations for writing this book. That anyone who reads this book will experience and enjoy the favor of God. The favor of God is available for all of us.

"For the eyes of the Lord run to and fro throughout the whole earth, to show Himself strong on behalf of those whose heart is loyal to Him." 2 Chronicles 16:9

Then Jesus said to them, "When you lift up the Son of Man, then you will know that I am He, and that I do nothing of Myself; but as My Father taught Me, I speak these things. And He who sent Me is with Me. The father has not left Me alone, for I always do those things that please Him." John 8:28 NKJV

To be loyal to God is to Submit to His authority and obey His voice. So when you do these you automatically become a recipient of the favor of God. You will naturally enjoy the favor of God if you are pursuing what He instructs you to do.

God is looking for people whose heart are surrendered to Him to favor them. I hope He find you.

Put the Word in Your Heart

If you want to enjoy the favor of God you will need to start saturating your heart with the word of God. Your tongue is the instrument you use to plant the word in your heart.

The Lord needs you to put His word in your heart. When you do that you are favoring His cause. But if you don't you are favoring the cause of the devil. It's important that we will do that.

If Jesus is your Lord indeed, then He will have to be the Lord of your heart. This means that nothing else but His word should find a place in your heart. The word should crowd out the desires of this life and the deceitfulness of riches.

You can only be a friend of God like Abraham when His word has taken over your heart. That way every word that proceeds from your mouth will be God's word.

Let not mercy and truth forsake you; bind them around your neck, write them on the tablet of your heart. And so find favor and high esteem in the sight of God and man. Proverbs 3:3-4 NKJV

Let them shout for joy and be glad, who favor my righteous cause; and let them say continually, "Let the Lord be magnified, who has pleasure in the prosperity of His servant." Psalm 35:27 NKJV

You will arise and have mercy on Zion; for the time to favor her, yes, the set time, has come. For your servants take pleasure ion her stones, and show favor to her dust. Psalms 102:13-14 NKJV

Those who commit to planting the word of God will continually bear the fruit of the kingdom for God. As a result they will keep enjoying the favor of God.

Commit To Growing

Jesus enjoyed favor with God and man because He was constantly growing in wisdom and getting strong in the spirit. As you grow in faith, you will enjoy the favor of God.

Growing is a function of knowledge of God. You are going to multiply the favor you enjoy when you increase your knowledge in the word. God will multiply His favor and peace over you when you increase in knowledge of Him.

The word of God is able to build you up, help you grow, so you can become a part of people who enjoy the favor of God.

And the Child grew and became strong in spirit, filled with wisdom; and the grace of God was upon Him. And Jesus increased in wisdom and stature, and in favor with God and men. Luke 2:52 NKJV

"So now, brethren, I commend you to God and to the word of His grace, which is able to build you up and give you an inheritance among all those who are sanctified. Acts 20:32 NNKJV

Favor is for the mature in Christ. If you are not growing from being a child to being a son of God, you will not enjoy the favor of God. God;'s favor is not for babes in Christ but for the mature.

Please God

Jesus enjoyed God's favor because He always did everything to please God. We can only bring God pleasure through faith. We all want to favor anyone who bring us pleasure.

Herod gave the young lady the head of John the Baptist on a platter simply because she danced and brought pleasure to him. Imagined when you do things that bring pleasure to God.

Those who continually operate in faith, will always enjoy the favor of God.

Now the just shall live by faith; but if anyone draws back, My soul has no pleasure in him. But we are not of those who draw back to perdition, but of those who believe to the saving of the soul. Hebrews 10:38-39 NKJV

When a man's ways please the Lord, He makes even his enemies to be at peace with him. Proverbs 16:7 NKJV

But without faith it is impossible to please Him, for he who comes to God must believe that He is, and that he is a rewarder of those who diligently seek Him. Hebrews 11:6 NKJV

If you do the things that bring God pleasure, you will enjoy His favor always. Believe God and take a step of faith and you will always have His favor.

Faithful To God's Assignment

Another factor that makes us enjoy the favor of God is our faithfulness to what God assigned us. We are stewards of the mysteries of God and we are to be faithful. If we are faithful, and committed to doing what God instructs to, we will enjoy His favor over our lives.

Who then is a faithful and wise servant, whom his master made ruler over his household, to give them food fun due season? Blessed is that servant whom his master, when he comes, will find so doing. Assuredly, I say to you that he will make him ruler over all his goods. But if that evil servant says in his heart, 'My master is delaying his coming,' and begins to beat his fellow servants, and to eat and drink with the drunkards, the master of that servant will come on a day when he is not looking for him and at an hour that he is not aware of, and will cut him in two and appoint him his portion with the hypocrites. There shall be weeping and gnashing of teeth. Matthew 24:45-50 NKJV

And he said to him, 'Well done, good servant, because you were faithful in a very little, have authority over ten cities." Luke 19:17 NKJV

Stay faithful with what God commit into your hands and you will enjoy His favor. But if you are given to frivolity and you leave that for something else, you will never receive His favor.

One favor from God can change your life forever. It's your responsibility to seek God's favor. It is time for God to favor you.

CHAPTER TEN

Seeking The Father's Heart

In 1979, a DC-10 Passenger Jet flew from New Zealand to Antarctica on a sightseeing excursion on Air New Zealand flight 901. This 8 hour flight would provide passengers an experience of a lifetime: a chance to see the bottom of the world. 257 passengers and crew members took off at 8:20 that morning for routine 8 hour round-trip sightseeing trip with great anticipation to experience a part of the world very few people had ever seen.

Unbeknownst to the flight crew, someone mistakenly changed the flight plan...typing a "6" into the flight computer instead of a "4" when entering the final number of the latitude and longitude coordinates. This simple mistake changed the flight plan by a mere two degrees...a very small mistake...but one that changed the course of the flight East by 28 miles on the flight to Antarctica.

While the pilots were both very experienced, neither had flown the Antarctic route. There was no way for them to know their new course put them on a collision course with Mt. Erebus, an active volcano rising above the frozen Antarctic landscape by 12,000 feet. The picture in the article header shows the change to the route of this ill-fated flight.

As the plane approached their destination, they encountered bad weather that made visibility difficult. Because they thought they were 28 miles to the West, the pilots descended to below 6000 feet so the passengers could see the terrain and the penguins of Antarctica. As the pilots flew on, the snow and ice on the volcano blended with the white clouds of the weather system and the pilots thought they were flying over flat ground.

By the time the plane's instruments detected the ground was rising towards them, the pilots had no chance to pull out. At 12:49pm, the plane crashed into the side of Mt. Erebus at 400 MPH, a tragic accident where each of the 257 passengers and crew members died. Air New Zealand Flight 901 is still the single-largest tragedy in New Zealand history, and the fourth-largest flight disaster of all time. All from a seemingly small, 2 degree mistake, only 28 miles in a flight of over 2,500 miles.

Experts in air navigation have a rule of thumb known as the 1 in 60 rule. It states that for every 1 degree a plane veers off its course, it misses its target destination by 1 mile for every 60 miles you fly. This means that the further you travel, the further you are from your destination.

If you're off course by just one degree, after one foot, you'll miss your target by 0.2 inches. Trivial, right? But…

After 100 yards, you'll be off by 5.2 feet. Not huge, but noticeable.

After a mile, you'll be off by 92.2 feet. One degree is starting to make a difference.

If you veer off course by 1 degree flying around the equator, you'll land almost 500 miles off target!

Fulfilling our calling in God is like an airplane journey. From the time you take off, you will be off course 99% of the time. Your will and flesh will constantly change the coordinates of your journey. The purpose and role of the pilot and the avionics systems is to continually bring the plane back on course so that it arrives on schedule at its destination. The pilot has to be in touch with the airport to stay in his part without getting into the course of other planes.

In life and ministry, you are the pilot. To reach your destination and fulfill your calling, you must do as a pilot does. You must stay in touch with God to know clearly which direction to take to reach your destination. He knows where your destination is and how you are going to get there.

For thou hast possessed my reins: thou hast covered me in my mother's womb. I will praise thee; for I am fearfully and wonderfully made: marvellous are thy works; and that my soul knoweth right well. My substance was not hid from thee, when I was made in secret, and curiously wrought in the lowest parts of the earth. Thine eyes did see my substance, yet being unperfect; and in thy book all my members were written, which in continuance were fashioned, when as yet there was none of them. Psalms 139:13-16 KJV

Just as an aircraft faces headwinds, downdrafts, storm fronts, wind shear, lightning and unexpected turbulence that takes not off course, you will experience the same in life as you pursue your calling. Many things will come your way that will tend to push you off the path to fulfilling your calling and reaching your destiny.

You will have people prophesy wrongly to you, you will be offended, you will get tired, you will want to relax and settle, you will be hated and maligned, people will abuse you and say many wrong things against you. In all of this, you have to stay focused on your call. You can only stay focused if you continually seek and inquire of God.

God knows you heart and your destiny. He knows how you are going to get there. He created you and have a call for you. You can only fulfill that destiny if you seek and hearken to Him.

When you have the heart of obedience, you will always be ready to inquire of God and obey whatever He tells you to do. Inquiring of the Lord will always lead us to obedience. Whenever you enquire of the Lord, you are seeking to know His heart and mind concerning you and what you are doing.

Even though Jesus was the Son of God, He had to enquire of God to do things rightly. He could have sought not to die, but He had to confirm from God whether it is God's will for Him to go ahead and die on the cross. It wasn't easy for Him to make the choice. He was human like you and I.

Now in the morning, having risen a long while before daylight, He went out and departed to a solitary place; and there He prayed. Mark 1:35 NKJV

So He Himself often withdrew into the wilderness and prayed. Luke 5:16 NKJV

"I do not seek My own will but the will of the father who sent Me." John 5:30 NKJV

What if Jesus had gone ahead and died without first seeking God, He would have missed God. That is why on our journey to fulfilling our destinies, we should continually seek and enquire of the Lord on how we are going fulfill the destiny.

When we make seeking and inquiring of God a habit, we enjoy course corrections as we go about. We all can miss our way if we stop seeking God to know where He wants us to go. Our thoughts and wills can lead us away from the ways and will of God for our lives. We must stay in constant touch with God to know exactly what He wants us to do and where He wants us to go.

Jesus made it a habit to daily inquire of the Lord what God wants Him to do and where He wants Him to go. If Jesus hadn't stayed in constant touch with God, He would have missed His destiny in God.

As we stay away from God, our flesh and will takes over. We gradually move away from the will of God by a degree. As we continue confidently on this new path, we continue to move away from God's will until we are far away from His will as heaven is far from the earth.

Door Of Hell

This was what happened to me while I was seeking the Lord about the next direction of my ministry. I was not really sure of what God wants me to do at that time. Someone, who was close to me who I rely on her words, came and prophesied to me. The prophesy was about a building and since I don't have a building, I felt like it was God speaking through her.

Instead of taking that prophesy to enquire of the Lord, I assumed it was a prophesy from God. I was seeking God then and when she spoke to me, I felt it was a word of God in answer to my seeking Him. I guess it was because that prophesy sounded good to my flesh.

I stepped out of my place and missed my direction because of the timing of the prophesy and the location was not what God have for me. It opened to me the door of hell instead of the door of heaven. The door of hell leads to suffering and challenges, while the door of heaven leads to joy unspeakable full of glory and abundance.

Obedience opens the door of heaven and creates the atmosphere of favor, prosperity, and God's presence. Entering the door of disobedience caused a lot of pain in my life. Through obedience I got to understand that I can never through disobedience enter the rest of God.

And to whom did He swear that they would not enter His rest, but to those who did not obey? So we see that they could not enter in because of unbelief. Hebrews 3:17-18 NKJV

Through this act of disobedience to the voice of God, I never got the support I thought God was going to bring me except from my elder sister, daughter, nieces and a few friends.

The first three months I entered into the building, everything went smoothly. So I felt like it was truly God. You know the kind of feeling you have when everything is all right. You assume it was God. I never knew that it was the calm before the storm.

So I decided to use the build for church. I invited people who wanted healing and deliverance to service in the building. Not knowing that the people I had invited, were like the people God has previously delivered me from. My disobedience was taking me back into a place of bondage that I have been freed from.

Paul advised us to hold on jealously to the freedom that Christ has gained for us through obedience. But if we decide to disobey God, we will take ourselves back into that same associations and bondage.

Stand fast therefore in the liberty by which Christ has made us free, and do not be entangled again with a yoke of bondage. Galatians 5:1

As a bird that wanderers from her nest, so is a man that wanders from his place. Proverbs 27:8 KJV

I thought it was God. It looked like God. It was too good not to be God. I thought it was God's approval. But it wasn't. I moved out of my place. The area wasn't the area God sent me to. My not being able to spiritually discern it as not from God made me think it was from God.

That act of disobedience moved me out of my place in God and to a place under the devil. That is exactly what happened to me when I disobeyed and will happen to anyone who disobeyed God. It is not all that glitters that is gold. That it sounded and felt like God doesn't mean it's from God.

I stayed in that building and prayed more to God. I cried more to God. I sought Him in that place. It was hard staying in the building. I was re-living my past when God had already delivered me from it. People tried to put fear into me, but I stayed steadfast in faith, fasting, seeking, praying and worshipping God. It helped me to learn to rely on God. The relationship I had with God brought me to a place to seek Him deeper for answers and direction.

It was a wilderness experience for me. Even though I was in disobedience and I suffered, it was also a time that God really taught me a lot and showed me where I was going. Even thought we disobey and are in the wrong, God is still faithful and His mercy endures forever even in our disobedience. People ostracized me and talk evil about me. I was betrayed, and persecuted. But God was with me.

Through all of these, the Lord sent a prophet to me who said God laid me on his heart. He said God will deliver me this month, which was September, 2020. That was when freedom and deliverance came over me. From then on, I moved into the will of God for my life. But I didn't close down the building till January, 2021.

I thought I was doing the will of God in that place, but I was really out of my place. There is no way I can do the Father's business and seek His heart in a place where He didn't send me and receive the harvest of obedience.

The enemy knows when we are seeking God for direction and he sends us someone who will prophesy a lie to us. And when we heed that prophesy, it takes us away from our place in God and opens to us the door of hell. We may think we are in the will of God as I thought, but instead we will be suffering. Every act of disobedience opens the door of hell to you. You will never get the best of God when in disobedience.

God was faithful throughout that time even though no one supported me. God will show you those who are His and those who are not. When you hear a prophesy, you need to go back to God to confirm that prophesy that it is from Him.

Whatever looks like it's from God doesn't means it's of God. People may look like they are from God, but they are not. The door may look glamorous like that of Lot, but it's not of God. It can only be from God when we inquire of God and know His will and get His direction. The devil can even pretend to be angel of light.

We are in a time when a lot false prophets will arise to deceive many and move them out of their place in God. Like the young prophet in 1Kings 13 who was lied to by the older prophet. His disobedience to God caused him his life. You should always seek God to verify every prophesy you get. It should be a confirmation what God had already told you.

For such are false apostles, deceitful workers, transforming themselves into apostles of Christ. And no wonder! For satan himself transforms himself into angel of light. 2 Corinthians 11:13-14 NKJV

Then many false prophets will rise up and deceive many. Matthew 24:11 NKJV

There are times when we think what we are doing is the best thing to do; it appeals to our senses. You have to be careful when it appeals to your flesh because we walk by faith not by sight. We are to inquire of God before we take any step.

Lot took the path that looked good but turned out to be the path that led him to hell. Abraham took the path that wasn't appealing to the sense and it turned out to be the land God promised his descendants.

And Lot lifted his eyes and saw all the plain of Jordan, that it was well watered everywhere (before the Lord destroyed Sodom and Gomorrah) like the garden of the Lord, like the land of Egypt as you go toward Zoar. Then Lot chose for himself all the plain of Jordan, and Lot journeyed East. And they separated from each other. Genesis 13:10-11 NKJV

There is a way which seemeth right unto a man, but the end thereof are the ways of death. Proverbs 14:12 KJV

Lot thought he had chosen the best part but not knowing that part will lead to his destruction. In ministry, it's not everything that is glorious that is from God. God's ways are not the ways of man. If God wants to take you up, He first takes you down. The ways of the devil looks good at first glance and is attractive. That is why many chose it.

"Enter ye in at the strait gate: for wide is the gate, and broad is the way, that leaders to destruction, and many there be which go in there at: because strait is the gate, and narrow is the way, which leaders unto life, and few there be that find it." Matthew 7:13-14 KJV

The way that leads to destruction is broad and many follow it because it is littered with gold. However the way that leads to life and fulfillment is narrow because it's unattractive. Only few people follow this path, but they end up fulfilling their callings.

David Never Lost a Battle

I have always wondered why David was always victorious in every battle he went to. There are many of us called into ministry that are living life far from being victorious. Did you know that David doesn't even have the Holy Ghost in him as we do? As sons of God, we are to be lead by the Spirit of God (Romans 8:14).

Ever since I learned the secret of David's victory and success in battles, I have never suffered defeat or entered into another door of hell. That chapter is completely closed in my life. Iniquity will not rise a second time. I am going the David's way just as I do the Daniel's fast.

If we want what someone got in the Bible from God, then we will need to do what that person do. We are to be followers of them who through faith and patience obtained the promise. They left the clues of their success and victory for us to follow.

If we want Abraham's Blessings, then we need to obey God as Abraham did. If we want to enjoy promotion and protection as Daniel had in a foreign land and have access to the secrets of God, then we need to go on fast as Daniel did. If we want to have the victory and success of David, then we will need to always enquire of the Lord before we should take any step.

Its good to hear direction from a man of God. But always make sure that you take it to God for confirmation. I made that mistake and suffered for it. Many have also made the mistake were not as fortunate as I was to come out stronger in God.

Whatever David wanted to do, He first enquire of the Lord by Himself. He doesn't take things for granted. He knows that his mind is too small to lead him. The way God led him last time cannot and shouldn't be used for another battle. He has to continually seek God afresh. This requires abiding in God and having a working relationship with Him.

"Therefore David enquired of the LORD, saying, Shall I go and smite these Philistines? And the LORD said unto David, Go, and smite the Philistines, and save Keilah." 1 Samuel 23:2 KJV

And David enquired at the Lord, saying, Shall I pursue after this troop? Shall I overtake them? And he answered him, Pursue: for thou shalt surely overtake them, and without fail recover all. So David went, he and the six hundred men that were with him, and came to the brook Besor, where those that were left behind stayed. But David pursued, he and four hundred men: for two hundred abode behind, which were so faint that they could not go over the brook Besor. 1 Samuel 23:8-10 KJV

You don't enquire once and for all. You keep enquiring each time you have to take a step to do anything. When someone prophesy over you, go to God and inquire about it. You are safer that way.

Isaac Experience 3 Dimensional Prosperity

Even though I was in a tough place as a result of my disobedience to God, I didn't relent in seeking God and asking Him what I should do. God will never give up on you no matter how far you have gone on the path of disobedience. His Spirit will continue to woe you back to His heart. His heart is filled with love for you.

When I look at where I am now and what is happening in my life, I can trace it back to how I sought God in that wrong place. I sought Him like my whole life depended on it; and the truth is that it did.

It reminds me of Isaac and how God prospered Him. He was in a land where there was famine and drought. Nothing was working. He decided he was going to head to Egypt as his father, Abraham, had done previously. But then he decided to enquire of the Lord about this decision. He looked at the circumstance and wanted to leave, but God looked at his destiny and calling and told him to stay.

He decided to obey God. He jettisoned the idea of leaving. It would have been disobedience to God. I have prospered more since I closed that building. I have made more progress in ministry since then and I have more peace too. Now I know my obedience has brought me deeper into the center of God's will for my life.

Isaac was right to consider the circumstance. He had families to take care of. However, he did the right thing by seeking the heart of God to know what God wanted him to do. And the moment God told him what His heart was, Isaac sowed in the land in obedience. He reaped in that same year what I call, "The 3 Dimensional Prosperity."

And there was a famine in the land, beside the first famine that was in the days of Abraham. And Isaac went unto Abimelech king of the Philistines unto Gerar. And the Lord appeared unto him, and said, Go not down into Egypt; dwell in the land which I shall tell thee of: Sojourn in this land, and I will be with thee, and will bless thee; for unto thee, and unto thy seed, I will give all these countries, and I will perform the oath which I sware unto Abraham thy father; And I will make thy seed to multiply as the stars of heaven, and will give unto thy seed all these countries; and in thy seed shall all the nations of the earth be blessed; Because that Abraham obeyed my voice, and kept my charge, my commandments, my statutes, and my laws. And Isaac dwelt in Gerar: Then Isaac sowed in that land, and received in the same year an hundredfold: and the LORD blessed him. And the man waxed great, and went forward, and grew until he became very great: For he had possession of flocks, and possession of herds, and great store of servants: and the Philistines envied him. Genesis 26:1-6, 12-14 KJV

The 3 dimensional prosperity is that Isaac became rich, wealthy and great. The Philistine envied him because of his greatness. I am entering into my 3 Dimensional prosperity because I inquired of the Lord and heed His voice.

When we see and know the heart of God, the door of heaven gets opened to us. I believe that anyone who has the heart of obedience will be a seeker of God's heart. You need to know the heart of God concerning whatever you are going through. When you inquire and know what God wants you to do and do it, you go through the door of obedience and enter into the rest and blessings of God.

When people see the blessing on you, they will hate and envy you. It comes with being in the territory. You should not allow the envy of people move you out of the will of God. Don't get offended, instead continually inquire of the Lord what He will have you do.

The more they envied Isaac, the more he sought God and commit to what God instructed him to do and the more God prospered him and made him great. This is exactly what is happening to me. You should not allow anyone distract you from inquiring of the Lord. It will lead you to the right place and in the right place, God will prosper you.

Obedience is a great rewarder!

Printed in the United States
by Baker & Taylor Publisher Services